RETHINKING YOUTH

A note on the cover illustrations:

The cover illustrations were painted by Coryn Littler, Didier Luximon, Cuong Nguyen, Dean Kalauni, Anthony Cocks and Matthew Peet (peer educator) who form Writers Block, part of the Contemporary Urban Art Project run by the Marrickville Youth Resource Centre, Sydney. It was originally intended that the illustrations be painted on boards at the youth centre. However, the offer of a wall by the publican of the Cricketers Arms Hotel, Surry Hills, was an opportunity too good to refuse. So, one very crisp and clear Sydney winter's day, Writers Block began painting this book's cover on a pub wall. The result: a vibrant front cover and a very happy publican.

RETHINKING YOUTH

Johanna Wyn and Rob White

SAGE Publications

London • Thousand Oaks • New Delhi

This book is dedicated to four young people who have
contributed fundamentally to our thinking and 'rethinking'
about the central issues in this book.

To
Michael and Julia
and
Hannah and Frances

First published in Australia in 1997 by
Allen and Unwin Pty Ltd

SAGE Publications Ltd
6 Bonhill Street
London EC2A 4PU

SAGE Publications Ltd
2455 Teller Road
Thousand Oaks, California 91320

SAGE Publications India Pvt Ltd
32, M-Block Market
Greater Kailash – I
New Delhi 110 048

British Library Cataloguing in Publication Data

A catalogue record for this book is available from
the British Library.

ISBN 0 7619 5521 6
ISBN 0 7619 5522 4 (pbk)

Library of Congress catalog record available

Set in 10/11 pt Sabon by DOCUPRO, Sydney
Printed by KHL Printing Co. (Pte) Ltd, Singapore

Contents

Tables

Acknowledgements

We are grateful to the contribution others have made to this joint project. Our colleagues in the Youth Research Centre and in the Department of Criminology at the University of Melbourne have over the years provided a supportive and congenial working environment. Peter Dwyer has contributed to many of the ideas in the book and offered helpful editorial comments on the manuscript. Dave Palmer provided constructive criticism for which we are grateful, and Anita Harris's research assistance gave the project a great start. Thanks to Evan Willis for his willingness to listen and to offer helpful comments, and to Sue Medlock for being there.

Introduction

Young people grow up in incredibly varied circumstances, with different priorities and perspectives. While 'youth' does not exist as a single group, there is an urgent task in understanding what is happening in young people's lives generally. In the advanced industrialised countries, it is clear that economic restructuring has not been sufficient to ensure jobs for many young people. And there is a growing sense that the life experiences of many young people in the 1990s have been greatly impoverished.

How young men and young women negotiate their futures varies, depending on cultural and national context. Similarly, 'race' and ethnic relations shape youth experience in ways which reflect historical differences in racism, colonialism and immigration. The position and opportunities of young people in society are ultimately shaped by relations of wealth and poverty. These differences in circumstances and outcomes are so fundamental, that the category 'youth' seems to have relevance only in the broadest sense.

Yet, there are obvious commonalities experienced by young people as well. Growing up, at least in advanced industrial countries, has become an increasingly extended and complex experience. 'Youth' as an age category, for institutional and policy purposes, generally starts at age 13 and continues until age 25. It is likely that in the future this shifting category will extend even further, at both ends. In many countries, the experience and meaning of youth is also changing as young people actively construct their own group identities.

1

Young people are growing up in a world in which local and national identities are being reaffirmed, fiercely guarded and shaped. Young people living in European countries cannot fail to be acutely aware of the heightened meaning that local cultural identity has. Although their peers in the 'newer' countries such as Australia and New Zealand may find such intense cultural identification and differentiation difficult to relate to, even in these countries, old cultural and political struggles are reasserting themselves in the form of the claiming of the land rights and responsibilities of their indigenous peoples.

At the same time, the use of new media technologies has brought the same consumer markets to young people all over the world. Although not all young people have the same access to consumption, the marketing of 'youth' through products such as music and clothing is widespread, creating a superficial sameness based on age.

Young people are also subject to various forms of education and training on an increasing scale, and for longer periods of their lives. Some societies (such as the former West Germany) have a history of education and training for young people as a taken-for-granted experience of growing up. However, now other countries in the industrialised world are also following this pattern, eager to make some form of education and training an accepted 'pathway' to adulthood. In this sense then, young people will have in common the experience of spending a lot of their time while growing up (to age 17 or so) in educational institutions, and many already do.

We can also identify certain common threads in young people's experiences in the failure of youth labour markets on a large scale. Young people's involvement in education and training in increasing numbers is not necessarily related to a greater appreciation on their part of education in itself and nor is it generally related to educational reforms which favour young people. Young people are often forced to seek refuge in education and training institutions because they cannot find work. Part-time work is ubiquitous.

Increasingly, however, youth researchers have pointed out that the appearance of commonality is superficial only. Even in the same locality, social divisions will make the seemingly common experience of schooling or establishing a livelihood very different and the outcomes may be significantly different. Although social change (especially in the use of technology to enhance 'communication' and to bring about workplace restructuring) has affected many dimensions of people's lives, the strength of older patterns of social relationships is revealed by the continuing relevance of gender, class and ethnicity/'race'.

The aim of this book is to offer a *perspective* on youth which takes these complexities into account, drawing on the wide and increasingly sophisticated field of youth research which contributes to a 'rethinking of youth'. The tension between the apparent universality of youth and the highly specific, differentiated and socially divided nature of youth which we have drawn attention to is a central issue. Another important issue is the extent to which young people are seen as citizens in their own right rather than as 'incomplete' adults whose rights can be ignored. These are important issues for researchers, for those involved in policy-making and for those who work with young people.

Understanding the realities of young people's lives is not just a question of having the right research instruments. There is a fundamental question about the approach, framework or perspective that is taken. A perspective that gives visibility to the relations of social division in relation to young people might look like a prism, which changes the relations between the central elements with each specific situation (or movement of the prism), but in which the elements retain a presence (Wilson & Wyn 1987). In a similar vein, Chisholm (1990) has suggested that a Rubic cube offers a useful visual analogy to the kind of theoretical approach needed to fully grasp the significance and experience of 'youth'. She suggests that a framework for understanding 'youth' must include both continuity and change, relations of age and of generation, and the social divisions of class, gender, ethnicity and 'race'.

Furthermore, developing an understanding of youth which is based on the reality of young people's lives requires the researcher to take an approach that moves beyond 'discipline' boundaries, and beyond the dualities that are imposed by traditional disciplines, to focus more on the connections and links between different aspects of young people's lives. The links between 'public' and 'private' spheres, for example, are central to understanding the differences that appear between young men's and young women's orientations to the future. There are also very significant social processes that link young people with older people in their own communities. Gender and generation for example, is a very significant relationship, cutting across age.

In other words, being a 'young person' does have real implications, but its meaning is tied to historical and specific circumstances and the ways in which relations of social division are played out. 'Youth' then, is an historical construct which gives certain aspects of the biological and social experience of growing up their meaning. To put this another way, everyone 'grows up', but 'youth' is a specific process in which young people engage with institutions such as schools, the family, the police, welfare and many others. The outcomes are shaped by the relations of power inherent in the social divisions of society. Each of the chapters of the book offers a perspective on the changing significance of youth and the conceptual issues that are central to understanding the position of young people in society.

Chapters one and two set the key conceptual basis for the book. Chapter one explores the *concept of youth*, its historical and its contemporary use and usefulness. 'Youth' is frequently used simply as a categorisation of people based on their age. In this chapter we look at the ways in which this approach limits analysis of young people and of the process of growing up. We conclude that young people do experience many things in common because of their age, especially because of the way in which they are treated by institutions. We argue that youth is most productively conceptualised as a *social process* in which the meaning and experience of becoming adult is socially mediated.

In chapter two we provide a basis for analysing youth as a social process by outlining the relationship between *youth and economy*. Here, we argue that social class has a central presence in young people's lives, and that therefore the concept of class relations must also have a central presence in the analysis of youth. Class relations, and other dimensions of social division, we argue, cannot simply be assumed from cultural practices, and nor are cultural practices simply 'produced' by social divisions. Class, gender and ethnic/'race' relations are historical and specific, and their implications for youth need to be analysed in the context of specific situations. An understanding of youth and economy is central to 'rethinking youth'.

The following three chapters—three to five—offer a perspective on three areas which remain central in the wider literature on youth: *youth development*, *youth subcultures* and *youth transitions*. Each of these areas is explored in the light of the conceptual issues raised in the first two chapters.

Chapter three focuses on the idea of *youth development*, which has provided a powerful legacy influencing contemporary research, practice and policy regarding young people. This chapter discusses key concepts deriving from the developmental psychological approach to youth, including the concept of adolescence and 'development' itself as an age-related concept. It also explores the concepts of 'individual difference' and of 'risk-taking', with particular reference to gender and race. It concludes that the youth development approach is central in legitimating the processes in schools and other institutions which systematically marginalise, fail or exclude particular groups of young people.

The issue of 'youth identity', and the relationship of youth to culture is taken up in chapter four. Exploring the idea of *youth subcultures*, this chapter looks at cultural formation and young people. It discusses the production and consumption of culture and the process of identity formation. This chapter explores the nature of the connections young people have with particular cultural forms and how this relates to wider social processes. Drawing on the wealth of youth studies and research on young people's cultural and sub-cultural formations in many different societies, we argue that while there are common themes, it is essential to distinguish the different bases, meanings and implications of youth cultural activity. Institutions are a key element in this process.

In chapter five, we focus on the way in which youth is constructed and structured through the institutions that 'process' the transitions to adulthood. Education is the key institution discussed in this chapter. We suggest that the idea of 'transition' has enjoyed particular attention recently because the 'transition processes' that are structured by institutions are seen to be failing to offer real pathways for all young people towards gaining a legitimate livelihood. The fragmented, broken and disjointed transitions to adult life also signal increasing divisions between those for whom achieving a livelihood is possible and those who become systematically marginalised. Our discussion of the processes of transition to adulthood reveals that there are now relatively few clear markers of 'arrival' at adult status.

Chapter six returns to the central themes raised in chapters one and two to discuss *youth marginalisation*. Working against the grain of the discourses of youth and education policy, our exploration of young people's lives has led us to suggest that the idea of a large, secure and homogeneous 'mainstream' of young people is a myth. The reality is that the social divisions that shape the lives of older people are also central to the lives of young people. Mostly, the effects of social division are fairly ordinary—reflected in the small struggles at school over 'discipline' (wearing uniforms, being 'cheeky' in class), the everyday harassment of girls and young women, the seemingly effortless and systematic failure of young indigenous people at schooling. These and many other examples are part of the process of marginalisation—not of an insignificant minority, but of a large proportion of young people—from schooling, from the labour market and from gaining an adequate livelihood.

In the conclusion we bring together the main arguments of the book. We offer some answers to the question: why study youth? We suggest that it is important to study young people's lives precisely because the process of transition to adult life—for each individual—reflects both an individual and a collective process. The very nature of 'youth' is the result of social and political processes through which social inequality is constructed and reconstructed.

Young people are important because they reflect the results of political struggles over the priority given to the public over the private. The emphasis on the accumulation of private wealth over public amenity and opportunity has a very direct effect on young people. In societies where the struggle to maintain a strong public sector, including viable public education, transport, and health systems (as well as other public amenities such as parks, swimming pools, sports facilities), has been successful, young people are able to experience 'growing up' without the worst effects of social divisions. However, where the struggle over public access to education, health care and the other fundamental rights to a civilised life has been thwarted, young people are the greatest losers.

It is important to study youth, because the points where young people engage with the institutions that either promote social justice or entrench social division are significant points of reference for every society. Hence, the study of youth is important as an indicator of the real 'costs' and 'benefits' of the political and economic systems of each society.

It is also important to recognise that young people are significant in their own right. They are potentially a significant political force. Young people will have a significant contribution to make in the institutions in which they have the most at stake. 'Student participation', which is currently more rhetoric than practice, will inevitably begin to see some real effects as more and more young people are forced to 'participate' in education and training systems.

In exploring the institutional structuring of transition processes and the way in which cultural formation and youth subcultural expressions emerge in different countries and in different contexts, our perspective is filtered by our own understandings of the experiences of Australian youth. The approach to rethinking youth offered in this book, then, is from an Australian vantage point. One of the key elements of an Australian perspective on youth is a strong awareness of the need to understand the 'big picture', of processes and dynamics that extend beyond state and national boundaries, as well as being aware of the specific and the local. We believe that this strength is reflected in the book through our inclusion of youth research from Europe, Canada, the United States and more broadly.

While many of the examples and ideas we draw on derive from these wider sources, inevitably our arguments are made against the backdrop of our knowledge of Australian youth research, policy and practice. These three elements have been thrown into a new tension. At both the state and national levels, educational *policy* is of the utmost importance to young people's lives. Yet, in recent times, education (and 'training') policy has been formulated on the basis of an economic rationalist agenda in which young people are only of value as an investment in the future and as workers of Australia's restructured economy (see Marginson 1993). They have come to be seen as the bearers of skills which will be capitalised on in the future.

The concepts of social justice and equality have been lost to policy—replaced by terms such as 'individual difference', 'equity' and 'human capital'—which fundamentally ignore the power relations of social division.

Youth policy in the 1990s has become increasingly subsumed within education policy. One of the consequences of this has been the tendency to portray young people as a homogeneous group, a 'mainstream' or majority who are distinguished from a supposed minority who are 'at risk' and who require intervention and treatment to bring them into line. As many of the chapters in this book reveal, the *research* does not support this view of youth. *Practitioners* are caught in the middle, as schools and community centres are forced to close special programs which have served a wide range of young people with special needs and they are increasingly asked to target the few remaining services and programs to the most 'at risk', who receive the dubious benefit of under-resourced and short-term 'interventions'.

The urgency of showing the connections between research, policy and practice for these reasons also reflects an 'Australian perspective', although these issues are clearly of relevance in other societies. The *processes* affecting young people in advanced capitalist countries are similar. Understanding the effects of these processes on the construction of youth is the task of all who are interested in young people and their contribution to society.

1   The concept of youth

Young people in the developed world have been the subjects of an enormous amount of research over the last 40 years. In general, this research assumes that young people constitute a separate and significant category of people: as non-adults. A central and recurring theme in the studies is the problematic nature of being a young person and the even more problematic nature of becoming adult. Much of the literature about youth has inherited assumptions from developmental psychology about universal stages of development, identity formation, normative behaviour and the relationship between social and physical maturation. Yet very little work has been done to clarify the theoretical basis of this categorisation based on age.

From time to time this point has been made by youth researchers. In 1968, Allen argued that the concept of youth needed to be reassessed. She pointed out that, 'it is not the relations between ages that creates change or stability in society, but change in society which explains relations between different ages' (1968, p. 321). Twenty years later, Jones took up the challenge, pointing out that the sociology of youth was yet to develop a conceptual framework for understanding both the transitions young people pass through as they become adult and the different experiences of young people from different social groups. She argued that it is 'misleading to emphasise the qualities or otherwise of "Youth" per se, since the young are neither a homogeneous group nor a static one' (1988, p. 707). Her conclusion was that youth is most usefully conceptualised as an *age-related process*. This means that the focus on youth is not on the inherent characteristics of young people themselves, but on the construction of youth through social processes (such as schooling, families or the labour market). Young people engage with these institutions in specific ways, in relation to historical circumstances. There is a growing awareness amongst contemporary youth researchers that focusing on youth as a process throws into question the very use of the universal term 'youth'. For example, recently Liebau and Chisholm (1993) have suggested that 'European youth' do not exist. Their point is that as nationally framed cultures and economies follow their own courses, young people in the different countries and regions that make up Europe negotiate very different circumstances from each other. They are shaped by both the material, *'objective'* aspects of the cultures and societies in which they grow up; and by the ways in which they *subjectively* interpret their circumstances (Liebau & Chisholm 1993, p. 5). Also focusing on young people in European countries, Wallace and Kovacheva (1995) point out that the experience of youth is being 'de-structured', because the significant transitions in life are less and less age related. They argue that transitions are no longer associated with any age or with each other. Education, for example, has become gradually dissociated from work, and leaving home is not necessarily a transition stage linked with marriage.

This chapter discusses the use and usefulness of the concept of 'youth'. The first section discusses the ways in which young people have been conceptualised, examining common assumptions about what growing up means. The second section offers a perspective on the concept of youth as a *social process*. It concludes that it is important to study young people because they are embarking on a process involving transitions in many dimensions of life, towards becoming adult and establishing a livelihood. Yet, increasingly, the meaning of adulthood and how it is achieved, marked, acknowledged and maintained is ambiguous. The period of youth is significant because it is the threshold to adulthood, and it is problematic largely because *adult status itself is problematic*. The third section explores popular conceptions of youth, focusing on the representations of youth in the media as discourses about youth.

GROWING UP: THE RELEVANCE OF AGE AND THE CONCEPT OF YOUTH

One of the most significant issues which confronts the area of youth research is the apparent symmetry between biological and social processes. Age is a concept which is assumed to refer to a biological reality. However, the meaning and the experience of age, and of the process of ageing, is subject to historical and cultural processes. Although each person's life span can be measured 'objectively' by the passing of time, cultural understandings about life stages give the process of growing up, and of ageing, its social meaning. Specific social and political processes provide the frame within which cultural meanings are developed. Both youth and childhood have had and continue to have different meanings depending on young people's social, cultural and political circumstances.

Research on young people's lives in non-Western countries exposes the ideal of the happy, safe childhood and period of youth as myths, 'built around the social preoccupations and priorities of the capitalist countries of Europe and the United States' (Boyden 1990, p. 184). As a stark contrast to the Western ideal, she poses the trafficking and sexual exploitation of children in Thailand and the Philippines, the crimes perpetrated on young people in Argentina under the military regime and the repression and detention of young people in South Africa under apartheid. More importantly, Boyden also refers to ethnographic research which reveals that children and young people are expected to work for an income in some societies (for example, in Bangalore, India), not just for economic reasons, but also because it is believed that they should engage with adult life as early as possible.

When a global perspective is taken, the socially constructed nature of 'youth' becomes more apparent. For a large proportion of the world's young people, the idea of 'youth' as a universal stage of development was and remains an inappropriate concept. In 1986, the International Year of Youth, it was estimated by the International Labour Organisation that globally:

> there are some 50 million children under the age of 15 who are at
> work. Nearly 98 per cent of all these child labourers are found in
> developing countries. The striking increase in the urban youth popul-
> ations of less developed regions has created the phenomenon of the
> 'street children' who live and work on the streets, doing anything
> that will earn them and their families that little extra which enables
> them to survive . . . If 'youth' is understood as constituting the
> period between the end of childhood, on the one hand, and entry
> into the world of work on the other, then it is manifest that youth
> does not exist in the situations outlined above (United Nations 1986,
> p. 8).

Although the experience of youth varies widely, and may not exist at all for some, the *concept* of youth is important in enabling us to understand some of the complexities of social change and the intersections between institutions and personal biography. We argue that it is most usefully seen as a *relational* concept, which refers

to the social processes whereby age is socially constructed, institutionalised and controlled in historically and culturally specific
ways.

It may be useful here to refer to earlier conceptual debates over
the concept of gender, because there are similarities. In the 1960s
and 1970s, the idea of sex roles was especially powerful in drawing
attention to inequalities between men and women. The concept of
sex roles provided a framework in which both men and women were
seen to become limited by socially constructed categories, or roles.
Although this concept offered a useful descriptive model, and was a
significant basis for educational strategies to address gender inequality (Connell 1987), it had serious drawbacks. The static and
categorical concept of sex roles, in which masculinity and femininity
were seen as simply discrete, if socially constructed, categories failed
to give any grasp of the *relationship* between masculinities and
femininities. Ultimately, the sex roles framework was replaced by a
more sophisticated understanding of gender as a relational concept,
which placed *power* at the centre. Gender as a relational concept
draws attention to the ways in which masculinity and femininity are
constructed in relation to each other. They are not simply 'different'
categories and they cannot be understood independently of each
other. Davies, for example, describes how the boys in her study
worked hard to maintain a dualism between 'boys' and 'girls' by
denigrating, devaluing and constantly drawing attention to 'feminine'
behaviour. These boys provide an example of the way in which 'being
masculine' involves maintaining a *hierarchy* in which being male has
the greater value (Davies 1993, p. 107). There are several useful
discussions of this conceptual issue; for example, Franzway and Lowe
(1978), Connell (1987) and Edwards (1983) have provided extensive
analyses of the limitations of a categorical approach to gender
relations.

Youth is a relational concept because it exists and has meaning
largely in relation to the concept of adulthood. The concept of youth,
as idealised and institutionalised (for example in education systems
and welfare organisations in industrialised countries) supposes eventual arrival at the status of adulthood. If youth is a state of
'becoming', adulthood is the 'arrival' (see table 2.1) At the same
time, youth is also 'not adult', a deficit of the adult state. This
dimension of the concept of youth is evident in the positioning of
young people as requiring guidance and expert attention (from
professionals) to ensure that the process of becoming adult is con-
ducted correctly.

Understanding youth as a relational concept brings *power relations* to the forefront. For the purposes of our analysis, this is an
important dimension in understanding the experiences that different

Table 1.1   Notions of youth and adult

Youth	Adult
Not adult/adolescent	Adult/grown up
Becoming	Arrived
Presocial self that will emerge under the right conditions	Identity is fixed
Powerless & vulnerable	Powerful & strong
Less responsible	Responsible
Dependent	Independent
Ignorant	Knowledgeable
Risky behaviours	Considered behaviour
Rebellious	Conformist
Reliant	Autonomous

groups of young people have of growing up. The popular image of young people presenting a 'threat' to law and order represents young people as more powerful than they really are. Although young people have 'rights' as young citizens, these are relatively easily denied, and they have very little say in the institutions in which they have the most at stake, such as education.

Another similarity between the conceptualisation of gender as relations of power (through the constructions of masculinities and femininities) and age (through the constructions of youth and adulthood) is that both involve interpretations of physical or biological 'realities'. The challenge, in rethinking youth, is to maintain a balance between recognising the importance of physical and psychological changes which occur in young people's lives and recognising the extent to which these are constructed by social institutions and negotiated by individuals. Importantly, it is also necessary to understand the extent to which categorical conceptions of youth have been central to denying young people their rights by creating frameworks within which adults can judge some young people as 'normal' and others as in need of intervention.

We would characterise approaches to youth which are based primarily on age groupings as *categorical*. The concept of *adolescence* epitomises this approach, because it assumes the existence of essential characteristics in young people because of their age, focusing on the assumed link between physical growth and social identity. For example, adolescence is assumed to involve a number of developmental tasks which must be completed appropriately or the young person will not develop into a fully mature adult. In chapter three we discuss the concept of adolescence in more detail.

One of the limitations of taking a categorical approach to the study of youth is the ahistorical and static nature of this approach. The assumption that age is the central feature characterising young people gives insufficient weight to difference, process and change. A categorical approach tends to rest on the assumption that the similarities amongst the age category are more significant than the differences, taking masculine, white, middle class experience as the norm. It offers little grasp of the ways in which the experience of growing up is a process, negotiated by young people as well as being imposed on them.

A categorical approach also ignores the significant role of institutions and of changing economic and political circumstances and their impact on youth. The result is the tendency to present the attitudes, behaviours and styles of particular groups as normative and to underestimate diversity amongst young people. Furthermore, this approach takes little or no account of the relations between young people and adults (for example, in communities where there is high unemployment, in rural communities during recession, within elite families or in urban Aboriginal communities). It also tends to ignore the relations between groups of young people. Schooling, for example, structures competition between groups of young people in classrooms, as young people learn their 'place' in the hierarchy of performance. Relations between groups of young people are also structured through schooling systems. The privatisation of education also carries the message that some schools (and by implication, their students) are 'better' than others. In some states of Australia, where a large private education sector is well established, young people in private schools learn quite explicitly that they are an elite (see for example, Davies 1993; Kenway 1990).

In addition, a static approach to the study of youth as a category overlooks the continuities linking past, present and future. This shortcoming has the potential to be addressed in contemporary research that takes a 'life course' approach to studying issues such as transition from school to work. Kruger (1993) for example, demonstrates that a focus on youth alone may obscure significant continuities between generations of women, by looking at life stages in isolation from one another. A further dimension of the links between past, present and future is the positioning of youth (and childhood) as a reference point for future 'real' life. Youth is seen as a separate 'stage' of life because the time of youth is about preparation for future (real) life—adulthood. Although this dimension would seem to contradict the static nature of approaches to the study of youth, when used uncritically it reinforces the idea that young people are marginal members of society, awaiting their full participation when they reach adulthood.

The tendency to emphasise the qualities of 'youth' per se has been especially strong within the tradition of developmental psychology, which has influenced conceptions of youth which are used more broadly. Because we take up this issue in detail in chapter three on youth development, we shall confine our discussion here to issues covered in recent and current approaches to the study of youth.

SOCIAL PROCESS

There are many ways in which growing up in the 1990s in the industrialised world is fundamentally different from in the 1950s. It is important to ask what are the circumstances under which particular groups of young people make the transitions to adulthood? Although the concept of youth as a subject of research was associated with social conditions prevailing in developed countries following the Second World War (Frith 1986), it is argued that youth as a period of transition into adulthood has a much longer history. Indeed, a focus on youth has a history extending back much further, depending on how youth is defined. For example, during the late nineteenth century and early twentieth century, working class youth were regularly portrayed as a public problem, and besides regular media coverage, were the subject of sustained academic and government study (Finch 1993).

Mitterauer (1993) further argues that it is too simplistic to assume, because of linguistic evidence alone, that the period of youth did not exist in Europe prior to the seventeenth century. His study explores the possible bases for categorising youth, clearly demarcating between childhood and adulthood. He explores the historical validity of five 'transitions in status': leaving school, finding employment, leaving home, setting up home and marriage. Mitterauer concludes that youth, as a period of transition to adulthood is not usefully categorised in this way, because the timing of these aspects of transition, their meaning and their order of occurrence differ for young men and young women, and from one region to another, reflecting urban–rural differences as well as regional economic differences.

> Our analysis of traditional thresholds of youth has shown that many of them were applicable only to young men. This was particularly true of thresholds which had their historical roots in the granting of arms. Like these traditional thresholds, the concepts of youth which are based on them are primarily male in orientation. Male and female youth were so different that until the end of the nineteenth century the concepts relating to the age-group were entirely gender-

specific. Only then did a sexually inclusive collective concept of youth emerge. But even so, the turning points of the biography of youth continued to be very different for the two sexes (Mitterauer 1993 p. 87).

Youth, as a period of transition to adulthood, has meaning only in relation to the specific circumstances of social, political and economic conditions. Once this is understood, it is possible to bring social conditions to the foreground and examine the significant differences between groups of young people as they engage with the processes which will take them closer to adult life. Inevitably, viewing youth as a social process raises questions about the meaning of 'adult' status. For the concept of youth to have meaning its end point—adulthood—also has to have a clear meaning.

Historically, there have been periods when, for some groups of young people, the social processes were far more clear cut than they are today. For example, becoming adult for middle class male Australians in the 1960s was largely a process of getting a job, a car, establishing a career, getting married and buying a home. For this group, as for white middle class men in most developed countries at this time, youth and adulthood were relatively clearly demarcated by accepted patterns of consumption and production. The concept of youth as a distinct category, within a finite time span, fits the experiences of this historical group most closely.

Even during this time, however, the patterns of growing up on which the concept is based were not universally experienced. The transitions to adulthood for women were very different from their male counterparts'. Women's patterns of employment did not match men's. They were much more likely to remain dependent on a partner, or on the government if they were the recipients of income security. Women in the paid workforce were largely ignored by trade unions and by government policy (Probert 1989). It was only in the latter half of the 1960s that Australian women, upon marriage, were not required to resign their permanent positions as teachers. Their participation in the workforce, although increasing, revealed that women were limited to employment in a few sectors of the labour market compared with men, and they were not represented in the higher paid, senior positions of their occupations.

These examples illustrate that the concept of youth involves a tension between the social significance of age, which gives young people a *common* social status which is different from adulthood, and the social significance of other social divisions, which *differentiate* young people from each other. Table 2.2 draws attention to this point, in terms of the contradiction between homogeneity and heterogeneity in the concept of youth.

Table 1.2   Universal and particular elements in the conception of youth

Universal	Particular
Age status	Social status, e.g., class, gender, ethnicity, 'race', geographical location
Global youth culture	Cultural formation, e.g., youth subcultures
Compulsory schooling	Unequal provision, opportunities and outcomes
Legal prescriptions based on age, e.g., status offences	State regulation according to social status, e.g., indigenous young people and police
Adolescent development	Diverse life experiences and cultural norms for growing up
Youth as deficient	Youth as having multiple dimensions

While young people do have a common status and to some extent common experiences (for example, schooling) because of their age, there are many 'forces' which work against this. For example, researchers are now beginning to provide evidence that the experiences of older people in the labour market and in the home have a strong impact on the visions young people have of their own futures. This means that gender divisions and inequalities continue to have a powerful impact on the way in which young men and women approach the decisions which will affect their futures. Despite nearly 20 years of equal opportunity reform in Australian schooling, for example, young women continue to make decisions about their future lives in terms of very different priorities from young men. Young women accept that it is possible for women to challenge the occupational boundaries of the gender-segmented labour market, but many are reluctant to do so, because they envisage their futures as adults in terms of balancing paid and unpaid labour and public and private responsibilities (Ashenden & Associates 1992).

Researchers in Canada, the Netherlands and Germany have found the same trends occurring with regard to young women's approaches to adult life (Looker 1993; du Bois-Reymond et al. 1994; Kruger 1993). Young women, even though they might be aware of the potential opportunities that education offers them to achieve 'equality' with their male peers, continue to make decisions about their futures based on what they perceive to be the reality, that is, inequality. These aspects of the transitions to adulthood are taken up in more detail in chapter five.

In Australia, young Aboriginal people of both sexes in the 1960s also anticipated a very different transition to adulthood from their white counterparts'. Even in the 1980s, the relevance of the term 'adolescence' for young Aboriginal people was contested. McConnochie (1982) argues that the category of youth, as employed by many non-indigenous researchers, is inappropriate to characterise the social experience of growing up for young Aboriginal people. McConnochie's reservation about the use of the term 'adolescence' stemmed from his perception that it implied that there were 'internal psychological traits' which could be used to explain behaviour. By contrast he pointed to the nature of the social conditions affecting many young Aboriginal people. Traditional Aboriginal cultures carefully prescribed the process of becoming an adult, leaving relatively little room for speculation. However, fundamental social change to the traditional life of Aboriginal peoples meant that both achieving adult status and the meaning of adulthood have become increasingly ambiguous and uncertain.

The idea that youth only has meaning in relation to specific circumstances is also supported by a consideration of class relations. One of the key conditions that young people have had to face during the 1980s and 1990s is *the failure of the economies* of most Western societies to provide employment that sustains the establishment of a legitimate livelihood for significant proportions of young people. The struggle to establish a livelihood, historically the special burden of working class communities, continues to be central (Wilson & Wyn 1987). In the 1990s, it is clear from the experience of New Zealand that economic growth can continue to produce jobs and improve the standard of living of a proportion of the population, while at the same time the conditions and life chances of a large proportion of the society can actually deteriorate (Kelsey 1995). Young people who fail to find employment that is stable enough and well paid enough to establish a legitimate livelihood have major difficulties now and in later life. These young people become marginal to our society not because of their youth, but because of the operation of economic and political processes. There is increasing evidence that activities across multiple economies (see table 2.2) is the only way young people can gain access to a livelihood that is sustaining, if not legitimate.

On a global scale, social and economic changes which affect remote, small-scale and large urban communities alike have a significant impact on the meaning and experience of 'growing up'. Although the impact of these changes is far reaching, it does not mean that the outcomes for young people are all the same. As this discussion has begun to point out, the social processes which affect the experience of growing up serve to differentiate groups of young people from each other, sharpening and reinforcing deeper social divisions rather than breaking them down. This discussion of social process has attempted to outline some of the issues that processes of social change raise for a conceptualisation of youth. Subsequent chapters take up issues raised here in more substance.

POPULAR CONCEPTIONS

Our discussion of the concept of youth would be incomplete without a consideration of the contribution of popular conceptions. The idea that youth constitutes a significant and distinct category is inevitably reinforced by popular media. Indeed, the analysis of media representations of young people occupies a distinct place within youth research. It is widely argued that in the 1950s, as patterns of consumption and production changed to give groups of working class young men greater leisure time and more buying power, the popular media (mainly newspapers) were involved in the presentation of particular constructions of young people (mostly young working class men). The term 'youth' became widely used in the 1950s in industrialised countries, as the experience of growing up responded to changing economic and political processes.

Frith (1986) argues that the term 'youth' was initially most frequently used in research on young men from working class backgrounds, mainly in the United States and in Britain. Relatively high rates of employment gave this group unprecedented disposable income, enabling them to use their leisure time in new ways, and giving them both a visibility and a form of power (Stratton 1993). Youth became a 'new category' of person, distinctive, usually male, and a potential threat to the stability of society. Although the sense of threat implied physical threat, there was also a sense in which young people were seen to symbolise change to moral and cultural values as well. This sense of threat was described by Cohen (1972) as precipitating 'moral panics' about the violent or disruptive behaviour of youth.

Historical analyses of the popular representations of young people in Australia before the 1950s, however, suggest that it is important to recognise the continuity of popular discourses about youth. In contrast to the historical evidence of considerable diversity in young people's lives, several themes in popular conceptions of youth have dominated. Bessant (1993) has summed up these themes in a recent discussion of the 'cultures' of young Australians in the years between 1900 and 1950. She discusses the dual popular representations of young people: as threat and inherently bad; and at the same time as the focus of hope and optimism and intrinsically good but vulnerable.

This discourse rested, Bessant argues, on the assumption that young people were naturally rather animalistic and uncontrollable, but that if tamed by social conventions they could be respectable. The assumption of this dual representation (of which the more negative image was dominant), provided an ongoing legitimation for state intervention, control and protection. As many researchers have pointed out, the youth who were represented in this way were almost exclusively male. These discourses also both drew on and fed the newly developing psychological theories which assumed that young people needed to pass through a series of developmental stages in which they defied the conventions of society and experienced a time of storm and stress, emerging from this process having 'found themselves'.

Subsequent analyses of later post-1950s popular conceptions of youth in the media reveal a continuity with these early discourses. Newspaper articles on youth are inevitably about young working class men (and often, especially indigenous and ethnic minority youth) who are seen as a threat to the assumed values of a 'majority', because of their style of dress, their violent behaviour, their drug-taking behaviour, or because of their attitudes towards employment, schooling or political processes. Stratton's (1993) analysis of the media treatment of young people in the 1950s, for example, argues that the derogatory portrayal of young people as 'bodgies and widgies' was a dominant theme. As the analyses of these media representations point out, it is seldom revealed that the young people who are represented in this way constitute a small proportion of the young population.

In addition to being portrayed as a threat, youth are represented in the media as both symbols and victims of modern society. In her analysis of girlhood in the 1950s, Johnson explores this theme, arguing that the concept of youth provided the imagery for it as a a time of uncertainty, which although threatening because of its potential to disrupt, would be prescribed by the biological processes of growing up, leading naturally to a stage of greater stability and certainty in adulthood (Johnson 1993, p. 36). The insights of developmental psychology offered a perspective on youth as a time of turmoil and change, in which adulthood was reached after completing specific normative tasks such as identity formation.

Johnson (1993) has also argued that the masculine bias in the concept of youth derives in part from the significance that youth had in the 1950s and 1960s as a symbol of the emerging post-war, virile and self-determined economies and societies of the developed world. The fit between this imagery and the experience of white middle class young people at that time was close enough to maintain the myth, with the promise that the transition from youth into a secure

and certain adulthood would also be the process for working class
males. Johnson's analysis offers a useful perspective on the use of
the concept of youth in Australia in the 1950s. However, what is
the symbolism of youth in the 1990s? Now, the transition into
adulthood is into a world of widespread uncertainty and scarcity.

Young people in the 1990s are seen to face significantly different
circumstances from those of previous generations. Giroux, writing
specifically about young people in the United States, suggests that
'plurality and contingency' either mediated through 'media culture'
or the economic system 'have resulted in a world with few secure
psychological, economic, or intellectual markers' (1994, p. 287). For
Giroux, young people are:

> condemned to wander within and between multiple borders and
> spaces marked by excess, otherness and difference. This is a world in
> which old certainties are ruptured and meaning becomes more contin-
> gent, less indebted to the dictates of reverence and established truth.
> While the circumstances of youth vary across and within terrains
> marked by racial and class differences, the modernist world of cer-
> tainty and order that has traditionally policed, contained, and
> insulated such difference has given way to a shared postmodern cul-
> ture in which representational borders collapse into new hybridised
> forms of cultural performance, identity and political agency (1994,
> pp. 287–8).

Giroux's analysis suggests that popular conceptions of youth in
the media not only represent youth, but actively construct the
experience and meaning of youth, offering a frame of reference that
may replace traditional frameworks.

In the 1990s, we argue, popular conceptions of youth continue
to portray the dualism of young people as both the symbol of
society's future and its victims, 'at risk' of succumbing to lives of
violence, drug dependence and moral degeneracy. In the 1990s, the
symbolic representation of youth lies in the areas described by Giroux
above as 'cultural performance, identity and political agency'. Instead
of symbolising the certainty of reaching the defined status of adulthood, youth in the 1990s, as portrayed in popular conceptions,
symbolises the use of new forms of consumption. For those who can
afford them, the technologies are now available to modify, shape or
transform the body, so that young people can become 'perfect' and
old people can look young. 'Youth' now has symbolic value as the
'outcome' of the process of becoming more and more in control over
one's body.

The changing symbolic representation of youth has meaning and
value in an increasingly global way, in a world in which traditional
boundaries are eroded. The traditional markers of the end of youth

are less and less meaningful. The implication of this is that youth as a social experience can be continuously available, regardless of age—the 'becoming' can go on and on. Youth, then, has symbolic meaning as an item of consumption. Of course, this symbolic representation of youth does not mean that everyone, or even a majority of people experience this. It is enough for highly visible media personalities to keep coming back, 'younger' than they were the first time around.

'Youth' as a symbol of consumption does, in a paradoxical way challenge the concept of youth as an age category. This emerging meaning of 'youth' means 'appearance', rather than age as such. The symbolic value of the concept of youth in the 1990s, then, is of youth as the future of society, not in the sense of the 1950s when coming to maturity was the imagery, but in the sense of having access to the trappings of youth throughout life, through consumption, and through performance. The symbolic meaning of youth, then, is not 'coming of age', but 'being anything you want to be'.

In addressing the question of what is the symbolism of youth in the 1990s, it is apparent that, as in previous eras, there are a number of dimensions which are simultaneous. At the same time that the concept of youth is an emerging symbol of consumption in society, young people continue to be presented as victims and therefore as a problem. This side of the multiple representation of youth is discussed in the following section.

YOUTH AS A PROBLEM

The idea that youth are a problem to society, and to themselves, is a central theme to which the media and youth researchers alike return. We have pointed out that one dimension of popular conceptions of youth in the media involves the positioning of young people as a threat to accepted social values, and as likely to engage in risky behaviours. In this section, we discuss this dimension briefly, foreshadowing the more detailed treatment of some of these issues in subsequent chapters.

Historical analyses of the 'youth as a problem' approach, although acknowledging that it goes back to the turn of the century or earlier, usually focus on the 1950s, seeing this as a time when both media and social researchers treated the phenomenon as if it were new. The new interest in young people as 'troublesome' is often linked to the changing economic and social conditions and circumstances, and their impact on working class youth. In his succinct treatment of the sociology of youth, Frith (1986) argues that the increased affluence of working class youth created new modes of consumption, of leisure, and of distinctive styles of clothing and music, which were identified with 'youth' culture.

At the same time, the concept of 'juvenile delinquents' came into use. Johnson's discussion of 'troublesome youth' provides a useful summary of juvenile delinquency as a 'set of concerns about the activities of young people and their supervision by institutions or individuals representing the social order' (1993, p. 96). What Johnson's analysis makes clear is the integral link between development of a discourse of youth as a problem, and the establishment of many levels of institutions and processes for the monitoring, processing and surveillance of young people (see also Cunneen & White 1995). While these institutions (schools, social welfare organisations and the juvenile justice system, for example) were increasingly charged with a responsibility for young people, this role was seen to be complementary to and possibly in support of family life. However, signs of failure to develop appropriately were to be dealt with by interventions of experts in the lives of children or their parents. The monitoring of young people has inevitably led to the idea that some young people can be identified as 'at risk' (of a variety of things, including not developing through the assumed stages of adolescence properly or failing school).

This concept plays a key role in positioning young people as a problem. There are many variants of the discourse of 'at risk', but most involve the following elements. It is assumed that not all young people are a problem, only a group who are not growing up in the way that they should. This problem group is identified as different in identifiable ways from an assumed mainstream of young people, either in terms of psychological characteristics (such as learning difficulties) or social characteristics (for example, young people from single-parent families).

The concept of 'at risk' depends on the idea that a majority of young people are 'on target', making the transitions towards adulthood in the appropriate way. The concept of 'at risk' and its corollary, the idea of a 'mainstream', are central to a categorical approach to conceptualising youth. The assumption that an identifiable group of young people are at risk gives credibility to the notion, integral to most education systems, that all other young people are by and large the same.

The idea that some young people are at risk is also central to one of the dimensions of 'youth as a problem'—the idea that youth are victims of society, as well as a threat to it. In the last decade, the newly found affluence of working class youth has been replaced by the poverty of communities who are bearing the brunt of economic restructuring. With the virtual disappearance of traditional youth labour markets, young people who would rather get a job are refugees in education systems which were never intended to address these people's approaches to life or to education and which cannot deliver their promise of access to a better life.

Recently, this approach has re-emerged with the idea that the young are a 'lost generation' (Daniel & Cornwall 1993). Daniel and Cornwall's study of young people focuses on disadvantaged young people, presenting their perspectives on work, school and youth services. The picture which emerges from this study is of a group of young people who have few points of engagement with society, and feel that they do not belong. This group of young people were portrayed as a 'lost generation', not because of their own behaviours or characteristics, but because they were the victims of changes to and developments in the economic and social organisation of Australian society, which marginalised them.

The concept of a youth 'underclass' is also gaining currency as a concept which describes the victim status of young people who are marginalised from society. Some writers focus on this group from the point of view of behaviour, arguing that young people themselves, through antisocial attitudes and activities, are a threat to society. Others argue that the notion of an underclass is useful because it highlights the marginalisation of young people by society (see Robinson & Gregson 1992).

Both concepts of lost generation and youth underclass, although useful in drawing attention to the plight of some groups of young people, do so at the risk of sensationalising their situation. Both concepts are descriptive, collecting together groups of young people who have been marginalised from the major benefits and institutions of society, emphasising the hopelessness of the situation of this group, and at the same time rendering invisible the differences amongst them.

Critics of the concept of a youth underclass argue that it is too broad a concept to generate an understanding of the marginalising processes themselves, focusing instead on the results of marginalisation (Williamson 1995). This means that although the concept is useful in pointing out the severity of some young people's circumstances, it does not provide the basis for an analysis that would enable their situation to be addressed. For example, although they are both marginalised, it is not useful to place in the same category black teenage mothers with young white men in rural communities in the United States, because their marginalisation can only be seen as the same in the broadest possible terms. Although the effects may be seen as marginalisation, the processes creating these outcomes are very different, and their routes towards gaining an adequate livelihood are likely to be very different.

The construction of youth as victims and as vulnerable was challenged by the emerging cultural studies research traditions which suggested that young people were not necessarily passive 'victims' of society. During the 1970s cultural analysis of young people emerged as a strong influence on thinking about youth. This tradition explored the dynamic relationship between particular groups of young people and forms of popular culture, including dress (style), music, film and video (see, for example, Hall & Jefferson 1976). The work of people associated with the Birmingham Centre for Contemporary Cultural Studies (CCCS) was especially influential. Their work has been summarised in a number of places (for example, Jones 1988; Frith 1986), so it is not necessary to go into detail here. Although the work which is characterised as fitting into the CCCS tradition is by no means in agreement about the significance of popular culture and of youth itself, it can be said that in retrospect, this work has left an important legacy.

The detailed ethnographic studies of groups of young working class men which were generated at this time were informed by a perspective that highlighted the active participation of these young people in negotiating their lives, albeit within the boundaries of their communities. At the time, the concept of resistance offered a view of these young working class men as agents rather than as recipients of a dominant culture. In some of this work, the emphasis was on their engagement in class relations, rather than on age as such (Hall & Jefferson 1976). Others argued that it was necessary to examine the relations between class and age, and particularly the way in which age is a mediator of class relations (Murdoch & McCron 1976, p. 10). However, despite this, the studies emerging from this tradition have tended to give visibility to the practices, styles and perspectives of young men, and later, young women, reinforcing their 'difference' from 'adult society' (Taylor 1993).

This tradition of ethnographic research on young people has also provided a perspective on the way in which groups of young people take up popular media, not as mindless consumers, but as an expression of their resistance to the dominant culture. Many studies have presented the practices of young people in terms of subcultural styles of expression, which, in their everyday lives, subvert aspects of the dominant culture (for example, see Hall & Jefferson 1976).

However, critics have pointed out that the focus on the relationship of young people to popular culture has tended to underplay the historically specific nature of this relationship. The meaning of 'the dominant culture', the extent to which it is contested and the form this takes are related to social divisions such as gender, ethnicity and race. The expression of youthful self that is evident in the adoption of popular music by young Aboriginal people in remote Australian

communities (Brady 1992) has very different meanings and implications from its use by middle class white young women in Brisbane
(Gilbert & Taylor 1991).

Johnson (1993) argues that in taking insufficient account of the
different expressions and meanings of the relationship of young
people to popular culture, the cultural studies approach has taken
for granted the idea that young people have a 'pre-social' self which
they strive to develop and express through their engagement with
mass media. By 'pre-social' self she means an 'essential' self, which
exists independently of social relationships, and which will strive to
gain expression. Hence, although the cultural studies tradition offered
an approach in which young people's behaviour was seen as constructive rather than problematic, in some of its manifestations it
failed to challenge the categorical concept of youth.

CONCLUSION

The central issue addressed in this chapter is the contradiction that
young people do share in common their age, but the social, economic
and cultural significance of this physical reality is far from common.
The chapter outlines the argument, which forms the framework for
the following chapters, that a *relational* concept of youth offers an
approach to understanding the social meaning of growing up that
can take account of the diverse ways in which young people are
constructed through social institutions, and the ways in which they
negotiate their transitions. This approach problematises the meaning
of adulthood, a status which is generally taken for granted in
discussions of youth and youth transitions and development.

There are many studies of young people which offer insights into
the multiple and diverse experiences of growing up. Perhaps over-
whelmed by the dominance of the developmental psychological
approach to youth ('youth development'), few have explored the
implications of challenging the categorical approach to youth research, youth studies and to youth policy. The remaining chapters
of this book offer such a challenge, drawing on our own and others'
research to 'rethink youth', and to develop a framework for re-
searching young people's experiences of growing up.

2 Youth and economy

One of the main implications of conceptualising youth as a social process is that the focus shifts from young people themselves to the way they negotiate, contest and collude in social processes. The impact of poverty on young people, the marginalisation of school 'troublemakers' and 'failures', the transformation of the youth labour market in industrialised countries and the rise of global labour markets have a fundamental effect on the experiences of growing up. These processes have historically been central to the social outcomes for young people.

In our discussion of youth and the economy, it is our intention to give some idea of the significance of social division in young people's lives. In particular, the aim of this chapter is to explore the class relations and positioning of young people economically within society. It examines the processes by which young people's experiences and opportunities are shaped by wider structural developments. In locating the formation of youth 'identity' within the processes of social division, our discussion provides a perspective on the processes that systematically result in inequalities in social outcomes.

The chapter provides an overview of class relations, and different conceptions of class. It argues that class gains its best theoretical purchase when seen as a relation and as a process, which intersects with other dimensions of social division, such as gender, ethnicity, geographical location and sexual orientation. We discuss the structural inequalities which shape both the opportunities available to young people and the process of youth itself. Young people face choices and constraints, and they are involved in processes of production and reproduction of cultures which are classed and gendered. In arguing that the presence of the concept of class is a central dimension in rethinking youth we are conscious that this involves 'working against the grain' to some extent. In her discussion of youth research in Britain, Chisholm uses this phrase to describe the necessity for youth researchers to take a holistic approach, integrating 'the public and the private, production and reproduction, structures and subjectivities' (1994, p. 2). As we have argued in chapter one, understanding youth as a process requires a theoretical 'shift' from a static, categorical approach to one which grasps social relations and dynamic processes. We now argue that understanding the relationship between class and youth is integral to developing this approach.

This task involves working against the grain in another sense as well. Youth policy documents consistently fail to acknowledge the significance of class. For example, Watson comments that in the new educational settlement in Australia, social class is watered down to 'socioeconomic status' and the concept of equality is replaced with 'equity', 'a linguistic shuffle which accurately reflects the perspective of the new managerialism, for whom the removal of all "subsidies"—such as free education—is the first move toward their version of "social justice"'. In addition, 'working class culture' is simply referred to as a 'wider client group' (Watson 1993, pp. 180–1). In this context, a number of youth researchers in recent times have argued for the reassertion of the significance of class in understanding youth, (for example, see Connell 1994; Watson 1993; Jones & Wallace 1992; Livingstone 1994).

In understanding the relationship between class and youth, it is necessary to go beyond simply asserting that the structures shaping the social divisions of class, gender and ethnicity/race are simply there, to be 'read off' from cultural practices. Class relations are historical and specific, and it is important, in understanding the meaning and experience of 'youth', to locate particular young people in their specific history.

This chapter begins with a discussion of young people's experiences of class division and then surveys broad changes occurring in the nature of production and community life on a global scale. Economic restructuring has major implications for young people in particular, and this is explored through consideration of both changes in the nature of the labour market and the impact of marginalisation. The chapter concludes with a brief discussion of the modern political state, and how recent developments are affecting the state's relationship with young people.

CLASS DIFFERENCES

The struggle to achieve a livelihood is an entrenched part of life. How young people do so, and how successful they are, is fundamentally shaped by class position and class processes. Across the range of basic social indicators—health, education, income, literacy levels, employment chances, mortality rates—systematic differences exist according to class background. Class, in this immediate empirical sense, does not operate as some kind of 'external' social reality. Rather, it is integral to the processes whereby individuals interact, negotiate, contest and collude with the institutions of society (for example, schools, families, criminal justice systems). Young people who experience the worst effects of inequality can generally see what is going on around them. For them, growing up produces 'sets of contradictions which they must negotiate as they re-position themselves and are re-positioned within generational divisions of labour structured by class, gender, and ethnicity/race' (Chisholm 1994, p. 2).

We are facing a situation in the 1990s and into the twenty-first century in which the achievement of a meaningful, fulfilling livelihood for a substantial proportion of the youth population is jeopardised. As Jones and Wallace commented (1992, p. 143, referring to young people in Britain) 'young people are getting a very raw deal these days, constraints are beginning to outweigh opportunities in many more cases'. They refer to the increasing extent of unemployment, homelessness and poverty amongst young people and the denial of their basic human rights to food, clothing and shelter. The divisions between rich and poor, the 'working class' and the 'ruling class', are more than evident in patterns of unemployment, income levels, general life opportunities and decision-making power. Given that the vast majority of people, including the young, in the advanced industrialised countries are reliant upon a wage as the central means of survival, then the very high rates of youth unemployment across the countries of the Organisation for Economic Cooperation and Development bodes ill for the future (OECD 1993).

In many OECD countries the wage is now even more significant for the young because of the withdrawal or reduction of welfare provision, especially in Australia, New Zealand and Britain. In the United States, welfare provision has historically been negligible. Young people in other parts of the world have always had an important role to play in ensuring the family's livelihood. However, not all young people are affected by unemployment in the same way. Nor do our social institutions offer the same experiences for all young people.

The effects of class division and class differences, for example, are readily apparent in the widening gulf between young people's experiences of schooling, of part-time work while at school, and in their dress, attitudes and behaviour. Privatisation of schooling in its different forms, in places such as the United States and Australia for example, is strengthening the social divisions of class. Inequalities are also reflected in who does what after the completion or leaving of school, who gets paid work, who goes to university and who succeeds in the pursuit of material gain.

There is of course a strong relationship between class and the type of experiences one has of schooling. This is indicated in the following trends in Australian education. If we look at the figures relating to educational participation, we find that the age that young people leave school increases with family income. In other words, children from low-income families tend to leave school earlier than those children from higher income families (Lamb 1994). Secondly, in the Australian context, the proportion of young people who attend state schools tends to decrease with increased family incomes. Translated, this means that the poorer sections of the population tend to utilise government schools, while those children from higher income households tend to go to non-government schools (NYARS/ABS 1993). There is strong evidence, therefore, that income makes a massive difference as to whether and how long children stay at school, and in which school sector particular groups of children are concentrated.

Class differences in schooling are also apparent when we examine retention rates as well. Between 1981 and 1991 there was a general increase in retention rates across the educational sectors. This is a trend common to most advanced industrialised nations. In the Australian case, the apparent retention rates went from 28 per cent in 1981 to 67 per cent in 1991. However, retention rates in non-government secondary schools were substantially higher at 82 per cent (NYARS/ABS 1993). Retention rates in the elite private schools are even greater, with virtually total retention (Batten & Russell 1995). Increased retention rates can be explained in terms of a combination of financial, employment and ideological factors. The difference in retention rates can be explained in terms of class differences, as manifest in the varying capacities of families to marshal resources in the attempt to purchase a more certain outcome for their children.

Class differences are also evident in the fact that other indicators of inequality, such as poverty levels, have increased in countries such as Australia, the United States, New Zealand and Britain. It was reported in 1994, for instance, that a quarter of the British population in 1991–2 were living on an income below the European 'poverty line'. Later research undertaken by the Department of Social

Security is said to have shown that nearly one-third of British children were living in poverty, with numbers rising from 3.9 million in 1990–1 to 4.1 million (Waterhouse 1994). Meanwhile, the same DSS report pointed out that incomes of the top 10 per cent, after housing costs, rose by 62 per cent, but the income of the bottom half rose by only 10 per cent. Comparable trends have been noted in Australia (Catholic Bishops Conference 1992). For young British people fortunate enough to have been born into the former households, the advantages are clear. For the rest, the structural disadvantages and material inequalities mean that their life experiences will be radically different from their well-off counterparts'.

CONCEPTS OF CLASS

The concept of class is used in a wide variety of ways. It is often used, for example, to set various 'empirical' markers of economic and social life; as well it is used as an analytical device to explain general social processes. Table 3.1 provides a summary of the main approaches to class generally used in social-scientific research. It is important to acknowledge the different ways in which 'class' is used as a term, and to be conscious of the implications which each usage has for substantive analysis.

It is our view that class is best seen, from an explanatory perspective, as a *relation* (that is, class formation is relative to the means of production, and is based upon oppositional interests in society) and as a *process*. Structures of domination and power are dynamic in nature and constantly affect the formation of classes at an empirical level, although the basic core relation is maintained. It is not that the various conceptions of class outlined in table 3.1 are somehow wrong or incorrect, but simple descriptive characterisations of 'social class', in either categorical or situational terms, do little to enhance our understanding of the dynamics of domination and subordination accompanying class division. They provide indications of 'class effects', not class 'structuring' (see below).

What is the significance of this for young people? Young people exist in the world as class subjects. This means that many aspects of their lives, including the construction of identity are shaped by their class position. This occurs on at least three different levels or dimensions of class:

1 *Economic*: This refers to the objective position of young people in the overall structure of productive relations, and in particular where they stand in relation to the means of production in society. For example, the family one is born into has enormous impli-

Table 2.1   Analytical approaches to class

Categorical

This approach sees class in terms of hierarchical categories based on 'social stratification' characteristics such as wealth, educational attainment, status and power. It is an 'empiricist' model which focuses on observable differences in socioeconomic status (SES) between individuals and groups. It provides a descriptive rather than explanatory type of analysis. It is primarily concerned with issues of social mobility and opportunity.

Relational

This approach views class as designating positions in a wider structure of relations such as the relations of production. Generally it sees class position in terms of the relationship of individuals to the ownership and control of the means of production, the expropriation of social surplus, and general functions in the production process. This conception of class is based upon the notion of intrinsic class divisions based upon one's relationship to production, and opposing class interests in the allocation of societal resources. It is primarily concerned with issues of power and basic economic structures.

Cultural

This approach looks at class from the point of view of human agency, where the collective experience of people leads to a unified consciousness and mobilisation against or in relation to another social grouping. In this conception the criteria of political/ideological consciousness is definitive of class. In other words, the subjective dispositions of people (i.e., how they think about themselves) is as important, or even more so, than their objective places in the system of social production or the socioeconomic hierarchy. It is primarily concerned with issues of class formation and class consciousness.

Situational

This approach focuses on the practices of individuals in particular historical or institutional settings. Its main emphasis is on the 'doing' of class, and is gained by analysis of the specific factors in any situation which together combine to generate a distinctive class experience. It examines the relationship between collective experience and the structure of situations, and in so doing attempts to provide an exposition of 'class maps' which take into account individual responses to social structural constraints. It is primarily concerned with issues of 'choice' and 'given situations'.

cations as to how one uses one's labour (for most of the population—a small minority do not need to sell their labour at all). In Australian society, for example, one class controls the process of expanding the profitability of the large corporations which dominate the private sector. This class, although it is a small minority of the population, owns or controls a dispropor-tionate share of the country's wealth. There are two implications of the economic basis of class for young people: the power relations in these processes exert a strong influence over the lives of those who sell their labour; and there are important differences in the way in which one's labour is sold. One of the reasons why so many Australian parents have been eager to purchase private education for their children is in the recognition that some jobs are better than others, even though they all involve selling one's labour. The existence of primary (full-time, secure) and secondary (part-time, dead-end) labour markets and the entrenchment of this feature defines an important 'division' in class experience, and offers a complexity in analysing the experience of working class young people (see Watson 1993).

2   *Ideological*: This refers to the subjective position of young people and reflects their personal affiliations and social connections at an everyday level. It involves a consciousness of commonalities with similarly placed people (for example, middle class neighbourhoods or ghetto neighbourhoods). People relate to each other on the basis of shared identifications, perhaps drawing from mass media images, but nevertheless based on similarities in life chances. In a nutshell, this dimension of class relates to how people think of themselves and their families and friends, and how they relate to each other emotionally, socially and culturally. For example, it has been noted in the Australian literature that young people in working class communities place a priority on 'applied knowledge' rather than abstract academic knowledge (see Wilson & Wyn 1987).

3   *Political*: This refers to self-conscious action on the part of young people in relation to their position as 'class subjects' in society. This is where people are conscious of their interests as members of a particular class. It involves more than simply identification with others of a similar background. It implies active mobilisation and action taken against or in opposition to another class. The development and fostering of class consciousness of this kind is part of an ongoing process in which mainstream institutions and practices tend to reflect the interests of the dominant class in retarding or inhibiting political class consciousness, while material circumstances and living pressures open the door to alternative, conflictual perspectives based upon class interests. Traditionally, the trade union movement has offered an expression of political positioning and a basis for collective negotiation of working conditions for working people. There have been major changes in the structure of work and the political role of trade unions. For many young people who are involved in the secondary labour market (of short-term contract work), the fundamental issues appear to be very different from those of their more privileged peers in the primary labour market.

In analysing the experiences of young people, it is important to grasp the nature of social change, and the profound impact this has on young people's lives. It is also important to recognise the continuities. While the fundamental dynamic of class relations remains the dynamic forged between the power of capital over labour, and the struggle of labour against capital, its meaning and its actual form is historically determined. In relation to this shifting class dynamic, it is young people in any society who are most likely to be directly influenced by changes to the institutional relations of power, and to changes in the balance of class forces at any point in time. The changes in and continuities of class society are of vital importance if we are to grasp the specific meaning which 'class' has for young people in the 1990s.

CLASS ANALYSIS

It is our view that what young people do and how they experience the social world is inextricably tied to very specific class circumstances. Thus, they are always subject to the particular limits and pressures associated with class location (see also, White & van der Velden 1995). It is important to bring class analysis to bear on the study of young people because class is so central to individual development and collective experience. Our intention here is not to reiterate the debates over class, and class analysis (see, for example, Wright et al. 1989; Jamrozik 1991); rather, it is to highlight the ways in which class can frame analysis of young people's circumstances.

Class circumstance can initially be understood as the effects of specific relations of production. For instance, those who own and control the means of wealth generation and production (for example, factories, television stations, banks) are in a very different structural position from those who make a living through the sale of their labour power (that is, wage-labour). The particular ways in which ownership, private property and labour power are institutionalised determines the different positions and capacity of people to marshal economic and political resources in society. The majority of people in capitalist societies are reliant upon selling their labour in order to subsist. As will become evident later in the discussion of youth and marginalisation, it is important to recognise that many people have now been excluded from the labour market, and thus the sale of their labour in return for a wage. Even those who are able to sell their labour do so under increasingly different circumstances than 20 years ago.

It is essential to distinguish between class as a position and class as a relation. Each aspect of class analysis is important, but is part of an integral whole. For example, the capitalist class cannot be understood only in terms of who actually comprises it (for example, predominantly wealthy white men), but in terms of the relations it embodies (that is, ownership, control and exploitation of non-owners). If we see things this way, then the issue is how particular social relations are reproduced in society, and how constructing the processes and content of 'youth' in particular ways contribute to this.

Furthermore, we need to explain social phenomena in wider societal terms rather than simply by reference to young people themselves and the empirical trends and processes closely or exclusively associated with young people. It can be acknowledged, for example, that regardless of the 'age boundary problem' (whether 'youth' is defined in terms of 12–18, 12–25 or 15–21 depending upon the institution), the notion of 'youth' does have real material effects—legally, economically, socially and industrially. Thus, while the age boundary may be socially constructed, it nevertheless is a significant factor in the lives of all young people.

However, to say that 'age' acts as an empirical marker of difference, and that it is a significant *social attribute*, is not the same as saying that age is in itself *socially determinant* in terms of shaping the basic contours of society. For this we need concepts which fully express the essential social relations and power structures of a society. The question is how does 'age' relate to the overall conceptualisation and institutionalisation of youth-related processes, and how does it impinge upon individual and collective experiences of becoming an adult. To take an example, extending the time that it takes to become 'educated' is in itself a significant issue for young people. However, even more significant is the way in which education 'sorts' young people into the 'pathways' that will lead them into very different parts of the labour market. The kind of work that Willis' 'lads' were aiming to get on the factory floor is now largely only of historical relevance (Willis 1977). Economic restructuring has reshaped the experience of class and work, undermining the strengths that 'shop floor culture' may have provided for men. At the same time, however, the changes in workplace organisation and the use of new technologies have confirmed gender divisions in workplaces, reaffirming and reshaping old divisions in new forms (see Probert & Wilson 1993).

In analysing class relations, it is clear that it is important to take account of the historically specific ways in which they work. While there is significant and at times dramatic change in the fundamental relations of class, especially those associated with labour practices, there are also significant continuities. One of the most important of these is that we cannot explain the situation of the poor (for example, as an effect of class inequality), without understanding the relationship between rich and poor (for example, as a structural relation of class exploitation).

To take a concrete example, in the area of juvenile justice it is often observed that young offenders share the same basic background characteristics: single, urban-living, male, high residential mobility, unemployed, minority group status, weak attachment to school or poor school performance (see Braithwaite 1989; Gottfriedson & Hirschi 1990). However, in the terms outlined above, we can say that these factors are best seen as the effects of class division, rather than the causes of juvenile offending per se (see Cunneen & White 1995). That is, the material circumstances of these young people are linked to wider class (and gender and ethnic) processes in society, which then influence both their immediate behaviour and activities in relation to criminality, and the response of the state from the point of view of predicted state intervention in their lives.

Class structuring in relation to young people is first and foremost reflected in the position of their parents within the overall system of class relations. That is, parental experiences of class and their objective position in production shape the economic, cultural and social resources available to children and young people. In material terms, this translates into clear differences with regard to location and type of housing, educational facilities and opportunities, and labour market participation and career prospects (see Graycar & Jamrozik 1989). The various transitions which young people experience, such as moving away from home, getting a job and establishing a separate household are all transitions which shape their social identity. What is important is that 'these movements take particular forms and occur at particular times precisely because of the class specific nature of the transitions' (Beasley 1991, p. 67).

SOCIAL DIVISIONS AND CLASS

Other social divisions in society (for example, based upon gender, 'race', ethnicity, disability, age) are not class-based divisions per se. However, it can be argued that the nature of these are shaped by the power relations of social class in particular ways. In other words, inequality and discrimination are, in part, sustained by practices and decisions based upon class interests.

Discussions of women's oppression (in particular, as this relates to domestic and paid labour, male violence, and processes of social exclusion), and racial and ethnic discrimination (with respect to immigration policy, cultural symbols, and lack of school and work opportunities for specific indigenous and ethnic minority people), need to address the different class resources within each of these communities and social categories. That is, social divisions which reflect unequal gender, ethnic or 'race' relations are themselves intersected by significant class cleavages. For example, ruling class young women and the sons of wealthy Chinese in Australia bear a different relationship to the social order than do working class young women and the offspring of the Vietnamese or Cambodian peasant immigrants.

The argument here is that the condition and processes of marginality are based upon a *conjunction* of structural factors. While 'race' or 'gender' oppression cannot be reduced to explanations which subsume this oppression simply under 'class exploitation', it needs to be acknowledged that the class structuring of gender, ethnicity and 'race' at the level of lived experiences is central to an understanding of economic and social inequality. The unemployed working class son of West Indian immigrants in England is in very different social circumstances from the employed professional African American, even though both may suffer varying forms of racism in their lives.

Another example of the conjunction of relational factors is shown in the way in which the form and expression of 'masculinity' may be associated with distinctive class patterns of behaviour. Gender is generally constructed in the context of a *hegemonic masculinity* which asserts certain dominant masculine ideals. The features of this hegemonic masculinity include male domination of women, the sexual division of labour, and heterosexuality as the single, dominant male sexuality (see Segal 1990). How particular individuals and groups of men—and women—relate to the dominant masculine type is influenced not only by biological and social-learning factors, but fundamentally by class processes associated with available material resources and specific cultures of masculinity and femininity. Of course, the picture gets more complex once we start to explore the variety of masculinities that are shaped by cultural, national and ethnic backgrounds and histories (for example, Greek, Vietnamese, Turkish, West Indian, Aboriginal, English).

The existence of the multiple kinds and dimensions of 'masculinity' and 'femininity' is increasingly being recognised and more systematically analysed in social research today (see Connell 1995; Segal 1990). What is significant about this research in the light of the present discussion is that gender construction is intimately tied to class processes. This can be seen, for example, in terms of how young men and women 'consume' mass culture (such as television, movies, videos, music), with differing types of feminine and masculine attributes being tied to different sorts of cultural production and consumption (see Johnson 1984; Stratton 1992; Blackman 1995). It can also be seen in the different treatment of young working class women and middle class young women in the juvenile justice system in accordance with separate images and behaviours of 'femininity' (see Alder 1994; Carrington 1993). Further to this, the nature of such gender constructions is changing rapidly in the face of transformations occurring in the spheres of production and consumption worldwide. What it is to 'be a man' and to 'be a woman' in contemporary 'global society' is thus fluid, overlaid by significant issues of material resources and social opportunities associated with class relations.

Institutions play a significant role in the practices of gender division. In a recent study by Carrington (1993) of changes in the field of justice administration in New South Wales this process is illustrated. This work examines the ways in which girls are punished by the juvenile justice system for simply trangressing the norms of sexuality, femininity and adolescence. In particular, the girls most vulnerable to expanding extra-judicial interventions (by social workers, psychologists and other officials) are indigenous young people and those from low-income working class backgrounds. The importance of Carrington's argument is that she demonstrates how the form and content of this intervention has shifted over time, and how the manufacture of female delinquency occurs under different institutional and policy arrangements.

The specifics and complexities of social process demands that we examine closely the actual dynamics of oppression in any given situation. It is vital in fact to explore the immediate institutional practices and trends which affect how people negotiate their worlds, and how social control generally is exercised. Analysis of youth culture and practices only makes sense in terms of particular experiences of class, gender and race relations. It is nevertheless essential to acknowledge that the different dimensions of sexism and racism are inextricably intertwined with the development and extension of capitalism on a world scale. The economic, ideological and political relations of oppression are thus inseparable from the context of capitalism within which they exist (see Williams 1989).

When specific situations are analysed, the outcomes can be surprising. For example, Chisholm (1993) has found that it is young working class women who are the most likely to challenge the stereotyped and traditional occupational destinations for women. This was seen as surprising because of the tradition of portraying working class women as the 'most' oppressed, as victims or as powerless. However, young women from working class backgrounds who are 'high achieving' position themselves very differently from their middle class peers in terms of gender boundaries. It may be that the finding which suggests that very little has changed in the occupational aspirations of young women since the 1980s will be modified if class differences between young women are taken into account. Aggleton (1987), for example, found that middle class young women made educational and occupational choices that reflected class stereotypes.

There are dangers in trying to pinpoint any one specific dimension of social division (for example, social class, gender, ethnic background or race) as being the only or exclusive definer of social identity or of life chances for the purposes of analysis. This is so for at least two reasons. Firstly, one's primary identity is constructed through multiple identifications (such as black, indigenous, woman, working class, married, mother). Secondly, identity itself is never static but is always shifting, relational and positional (Pettman 1992). Who one 'is' very much depends upon whom one interacts with, the basis for that interaction and the specific social differences and similarities between people. It is precisely this multidimensional characteristic of identity that has been the focus of feminist strategies to shift people's thinking beyond the oppositional dualisms of 'masculinity' and 'femininity' (see Davies 1993).

Having said this, nevertheless it is still the case that the effects of social division are most meaningful at a system level, and most profound at a personal level, when they are underpinned by particular relations of power. To take an analogy: prejudice (that is, attitudes of dislike towards another) is widespread insofar as many different groups have particular negative biases towards selected 'outsiders' (for example, 'I don't like Australians, they're too brash and loud for me'). But it is only when we add power to prejudice (for example, 'we don't allow lesbians into these premises') that we can really pinpoint the structural basis of racism, sexism or heterosexism.

Social difference in and of itself is not a problem—a plurality of experiences and ways of relating to the world and to each other can be a creative and desirable feature of any society. It is when difference is entrenched, and when it is premised upon inequality, that we can rightfully speak of social injustice. Yet, it is precisely this pluralistic notion of difference that tends to inform youth and education policy, rendering the relations of power between groups invisible. As Connell (1994) comments, in the 1990s the educational discourses about educational failure and success seem to largely sidestep the fundamental issue that it is people in *poverty* who are systematically the losers in schools. This is not just about difference, it is about the way in which 'unjust curricula' maintain unequal outcomes (Connell 1993, p. 48).

The particular types of economic, ideological and political practices in a society—for example, whether women have the vote, whether black men and white men can work side by side, whether gays and lesbians have a 'legitimate' place in the public domain—depends upon the nature of political struggle around issues of oppression (and the relative power of the dominant class and subordinate groups), and the ability of the economic system to sustain certain 'concessions' (such as welfare provision, equal pay, moral libertarianism) in the light of these struggles.

How young people experience their social worlds is fundamentally marked by their class background and their insertion into a particular pattern of class relations. The economic wellbeing of young people in a class society is dependent upon their ability to secure a wage. Whether young or old, Asian or European, male or female, conservative or radical, the fact remains that for all our social and personal differences, securing a livelihood within the limitations, opportunities and complexities of class society is the basic issue.

CLASS AS AN INTERNATIONAL PROCESS

Young people's struggle to achieve livelihood is connected to the transformations in the nature of production, consumption and general community life taking place on a global level.

There have been major movements of capital on an international level in recent years. This is seen in the concentration of capital on a world scale into fewer and fewer hands (witness the media industry), and the movement of transnational capital into every country, including and especially the states of the former Soviet Union and Eastern Bloc. The expansion of the capitalist system has been matched by an expansion in capitalist commodification. This is evident both in terms of institutional changes (such as the privatisation and corporatisation of formerly government instrumentalities such as banks, airlines and coal industries), and in regards to particular goods and services (including, for example, water) which now find 'value' in terms of their exchange for profit on the market (rather than in their immediate use).

In terms of broad investment patterns and commercial dealings, the main trade rivalries are between the advanced industrialised countries such as the United States, Japan, Germany and Britain. The 'third world' countries continue to suffer major debt crises, and have increasingly been under the domination of agencies such as the World Bank and the International Monetary Fund (IMF), which dictate how 'structural adjustment' is to take place (see George & Sabelli 1994). Private investment and private financial lending is generally seen to be contingent upon a country's adherence to World Bank and IMF project agendas. In human terms, this often translates into massive cuts to welfare spending, growing levels of unemployment and reduction in wages and conditions for workers.

The world is being carved up economically by the dominant economic powers—particular nation-states and transnational corporations. Intra-capitalist competition has seen the formation of a number of regional economic-political pacts, as seen in the European Community, the North American Free Trade Agreement and moves to create a similar trade bloc in the South-East Asian region. Simultaneously, international agreements such as the General Agreement on Tariffs and Trade (GATT) have been devised to both maximise transnational corporation control and entry into the global markets and to protect the privileged position of the dominant economic countries in the New World Order.

Recent years have also seen major movements of labour on an international level. This has taken the form of flows of skilled and unskilled migrant labour into new labour markets where capital has secured an advantage (due to things such as low wages, poor conditions, politically placid labour force, strong state control over union activity). It is also manifest in the flood of 'economic' refugees from countries where unemployment is rampant, poverty widespread and life prospects for the majority have been seriously undercut by a combination of famine, war, monoculture agribusiness and gross disparities between rich and poor.

The international division of labour has been associated with the ability of capital to go where the (cheap) labour is. This has increased the pressures on workers in previously 'protected' labour markets (for example, the advanced capitalist countries) to both secure and retain their work and conditions in the light of overseas competition. The result has been an ideological campaign based upon the notion of 'world's best practice' which has at its heart the task of increasing productivity, decreasing worker control and benefits in the production process, and ultimately lifting company profit rates to even greater levels (under the threat posed by enhanced labour market and product competition on a world scale). High unemployment rates across industries and throughout the workplace hierarchy are central to this process, as it provides the spur to 'sacrifice' on the part of workers everywhere.

Transitions in the nature of work have had important sectoral impacts. Thus, for example, the biggest losers in the employment stakes have been young people (see United Nations 1993). The issue is one which is not confined to traditionally depressed countries, but extends to all of the major economic powers in the world. Hence, from the United States to Germany, Britain to Australia, youth unemployment has burgeoned, with little prospect in sight of there being a significant downturn in unemployment numbers in the near future. The main casualties of economic restructuring have been working class young people—that is, those whose material wellbeing depends largely upon the sale of their labour power.

LABOUR AND SKILL

The effects of global economic trends and capitalist restructuring have major implications in terms of the requirements by the labour market for young people with particular skills and social attributes. It is useful here to discuss more fully the notion of 'world's best practice' and employer definitions of the ideal worker.

The 'ideal' worker is now generally defined in terms of qualities such as flexibility, adaptability, capacity for teamwork and demonstrated loyalty. Crucial to these characteristics is the idea that the worker be politically docile (that is, not engage in 'negative' industrial practices and especially union-organised activities), while being industrially multiskilled (that is, able to perform a wide variety of tasks across previous labour or job site demarcations). The emphasis on these qualities in the workplace has, accordingly, been reflected in the major training programs and educational institutions (see White 1990; Finn 1987).

The threat of unemployment has been used actively to create new expectations regarding conformity in workplace culture, and to instil a new discipline in both actual and potential workers. The contradiction here, however, is that while education and training have been sold as the means to the end of getting a job, the resources available for schooling have not been adequate to meet the demand. Furthermore, rising expectations which inevitably accompany an increase in the time spent within the formal institutions of learning have in turn generated increasing frustration among those young people who have 'done the time' but have not received a 'reward' at the end. Young people are often made to feel that this is their fault. But, as O'Donnell rather bluntly concludes, 'if people can't get jobs this is the fault of the economic system and not the education system, and we should not be in the business of merely trying to make certain individuals more competitive so that others end up in unemployment queues instead' (O'Donnell 1984, p. 170).

Ten years later it is clear that most education and youth policies remain framed within a perspective which fails to question the number and quality of jobs that are available to young people. On the one hand, the number of paid jobs has been qualitatively transformed by the fact that most teenage work is now of a part-time rather than full-time variety (Sweet 1983). Partly as a reflection of this, it is students, not the full-time unemployed, who tend to be the favoured group for hire by employers (McRae 1992). It would appear that having some kind of institutional connection is a prerequisite for gaining part-time employment.

On the other hand, the quality of the work available requires much closer scrutiny than hitherto has been the case. The issue of where young workers fit into youth studies research is relevant here, especially in the light of the position of most (Western) teenagers as 'potential' workers, and the institutional preparations to which they are subjected while in this status. It is not just a question of whether young people get work or not—it is also a question of the nature and quality of the work (Wilson 1992).

It is apparent that, regardless of the quality of education provided, there is unlikely to be a return to opportunities for full-time, secure employment for most young job seekers (Beasley 1991). Young people lucky enough to find work are subject to the same kinds of pressures as adults in the workplace. There are two, seemingly contradictory, processes which affect young workers. On the one hand, firms are under pressure to modify production systems in order to efficiently or more competitively create profits from the goods and services they produce. This requires 'the maintenance of a number of highly educated managerial, professional and specialised technical employees' to ensure the coordination and design of such productive systems (Livingstone 1993, p. 97). On the other hand, employers also require many other workers who are only needed to offer a much more basic range of skills, and whose labour is easily replaceable, and easily terminated, subject to the demands of production.

The result of these processes is that relatively few highly skilled young people are needed in the labour market, compared with those who are needed to fulfil fairly basic, and often short-term requirements for specific production needs. These contradictory requirements of modern capital, as Livingstone (1993) points out, make fairly difficult demands of our education systems. From the point of view of many young people, the situation is even more impossible. It is relatively easy in these circumstances to become 'too qualified' for the low skilled jobs that are in demand, and yet not qualified enough to be successful in the competition for the jobs that require higher levels of skill and which offer a more satisfactory livelihood. Young people are vulnerable to accepting poorer conditions and less pay due to general ignorance of the working world or to the 'catch-22' created by having to work 'off the books' if they are to continue receiving government benefits.

For those in paid work, there is enormous pressure to work harder for less and less reward, simply to retain one's job. Many young people entering the labour market find that they are exploited by these practices. For those out of paid work, the pressure is on to make ends meet in the context of a society where the wage is the central economic means of livelihood.

GETTING A LIVELIHOOD

The issue of youth unemployment and the dispossession of young people of resources and opportunities they need to 'succeed' in the existing labour market are of course central issues in much youth studies research. Marginalisation is often seen as an important component in many such discussions. We would argue that class relations are at the core of the process of marginalisation. In other words, the ways in which young people are influenced by class background, experience class-biased social institutions and develop particular relationships to the means of production (especially paid work), are crucial to explaining their marginalised status.

At a concrete level, marginalisation in the main economic sphere of paid work has important implications with regard to the activities of young people in other economic spheres (see table 3.2). Indeed, we would argue that any conception of youth 'agency' or choice must be placed in the context of the severe limitations on their income-earning capacities and on the opportunities they may have to pursue income-earning ventures.

The accompanying table details the issues confronting young people across five discrete economic spheres (see McDonnell et al. 1995). In most cases, young people are active in one or more of these spheres. Furthermore, there is much fluidity in terms of movement between the spheres of the formal and informal, the domestic and the welfare and the criminal. Young people thus may engage in more than one type of activity at any one point in time, and be moving in and out of different work or activity environments. What is most notable about these spheres is that firstly, young people are particularly vulnerable to exploitation in each of them (see White 1989), and secondly, the level and type of exploitation 'allowable' in each does not depend solely upon whether the activity is formal or informal, legal or illegal. For instance, a young person may well experience great personal hardship in a formal waged job, but feel much less pressured or abused in an informal 'cash-in-hand' work situation.

While there are benefits to be gained in each of the economic spheres (for example, money, a sense of excitement, completion of a task), it would be disingenuous to suggest that the positives of 'doing work' outweigh the negatives of 'how and under what conditions' this occurs. Likewise, it is simply unrealistic to suggest that

Table 2.2   Young people in the different economic spheres

Economic sphere	General characteristics	Issues of youth access and involvement
Formal waged economy	Taxed; state-regulated; measurable; sale of labour	Lack of full-time work; disadvantaged by lack of experience, skills and contacts; low wages due to age-related pay structures; harassment; poor working conditions; insecure tenure; inadequate health and safety
Informal waged economy	Untaxed, not regulated by the state, not measurable officially; illegal sale of labour; loss of award benefits	Normally employee/ employer rather than self-employment; low pay; insecurity and competition; open to exploitation and harassment without legal remedy
Informal non-waged economy	Not regulated by the state; not measurable officially; goods and services exchanged without money; difficult to assign value to labour; often within family unit; unregulated by formal or informal workplace norms	Hidden exploitation; unregulated hours; social isolation; infantilisation; power relations and sexual division of labour
Welfare economy	State income support for those unable to sell labour; not directly involved in the sphere of production; condition- based payments and subsidies; utilised by young people in education; training or unemployed	Stringent rules for claiming government assistance; poverty; cost of study; pressures to work in informal waged economy; inadequate provision of services and benefits
Criminal economy	Activities which cannot be undertaken legally in any economic sector; forcible redistribution of existing wealth; criminal activity can be informal or organised	Tends to be irregular; sporadic and situational illegal activity, predominantly low-level drug dealing and theft; supplements income rather than main source; irregular income; possibly dangerous; open to exploitation; criminal sanctions

Source: Modified from McDonnell, Harris & White, 1995

there are no qualitative differences (certainly in the long run) between the formal waged economy and the other economic spheres. The positioning of young people in the labour market generally, and in regard to these five sectors specifically, is precisely that which underpins a major part of youth identity and 'way of life' in the late twentieth century. As such, it is of utmost importance to them, and ultimately to government policy-makers. Paid work is a focal concern of most young people and is a matter of great social and public interest.

However, labour market policy on the part of the state tends to reflect the prominence and general interests of private capital. Simultaneously, however, the fiscal or budgetary demands placed on the state are great when the extent of overall poverty and unemployment is so high and still growing. One response to the financial pressures on the state has been to make 'unemployment' into an issue of 'unemployability'. This has been achieved by re-focusing policy attention away from 'job creation' and towards training and education programs.

Regardless of whether it is a 'welfare' or an 'education and training' response, the extent and level of funding by the state for such programs is a highly contentious issue. Again, this relates to the fiscal basis of government intervention and the political choices made with regard to the allocation of state funds. Countries and regions vary greatly in terms of the resources put into the welfare, education and training spheres. As much as anything, this reflects divergent histories of class struggle and differences in the organised power of the labour movement and allied struggles (for example, Black civil rights movement, women's liberation movement). Even where considerable funding is still provided (although the general trend is for cutbacks overall in the welfare apparatus of the state, particularly relative to funding for coercive functions such as policing and prisons), serious questions remain as to the content, outcomes and economic impacts of such programs.

An example is provided by Beasley's (1991) study of the effects of Australian government policies on young working class people's access to employment and training programs. Beasley found that there was a 'depressing' consistency in the ('unreformed') nature of policy concerned with young people's employment and training. She concludes that after 20 years of job creation and training schemes:

> . . . it does seem that Australian governments have consistently failed to produce any radical change in the social inequalities endured by the young unemployed. Indeed, one has to say that not only at the level of discourse but also in practice governments in Australia over the last 150 years and particularly in the last two decades have

consciously or otherwise acted uniformly to maintain both class and patriarchal divisions (for subordinated young men as well as young women) in their dealings with the young working class unemployed (Beasley 1991, p. 77).

Training schemes will not provide young people with a livelihood. It is also apparent that market forces alone will not be sufficient to ensure that all young people will have access to paid employment. The conclusion that is inevitably reached is that training and skill development need to be linked more directly to employment arrangements. While youth researchers have become increasingly more aware of the need to understand young people in terms of their specific location in class, gender and ethnic/race relations, this 'specificity' is seldom linked to understanding pathways to livelihood.

Establishing a livelihood is more than getting a job—it is about establishing a sense of belonging, of engaging in the adult practices of one's community. Finding a job is, for many young people, an issue of one's connections with the local 'employing' community. As argued elsewhere, close links with schools and local government and employing bodies represent one possible arrangement for ensuring that the initiatives taken by schools are consistent with policies for economic and social development (Wilson & Wyn 1987). In other words, creating real pathways for establishing a livelihood depend not on an abstract understanding of 'the labour market', but on a practical and detailed knowledge of how to link local education and training institutions with their immediate employing (or further education) organisations.

The other important ingredient in support of providing a basis for young people to establish a livelihood is the protection of *public life*. Wexler (1992) makes a strong case for the protection of public schooling as an integral part of public life in his study of social relations in three schools in the United States. His assessment is rather pessimistic:

> What I find in the school case studies are conditioned patterns of
> social withdrawal which challenge the basic constituent elements of
> social relations, or 'the social'. Instead of grand theoretical challenges
> to the concept of society, social, or social relations, I have described
> specific institutional processes that reverse the constructive or 'socializ-
> ing' (Touraine, 1989) establishment of society: instead,
> desocialization, or society in reverse (Wexler 1992, p. 110).

Wexler believes that the extent to which there is a failure to fully support public schooling in the United States, there is also a failure in society. Similarly, Yeatman (1993, p. 144) argues that maintaining the basic principles and structures of public life (in the centre of which we would place public schooling) is fundamental to the development of an adequate politics.

The prolonged dependency of young people on their families, and in educational institutions, is an argument for the strengthening of the principles and structures of the public realm in which young people can participate, contribute and, most importantly, gain a sense of belonging. The failure of the public realm is associated, for young people, with disaffiliation from the institutions which are meant to serve them, and with alienation from the society to which they are meant to belong.

The concept of alienation can be used to describe personal feelings of powerlessness, and the structural disconnection of young people from the mainstream social institutions. The link between young person and school, or teenager and work, child and family, youth and sports club are all important aspects of *social connection*. The depth and extent of social connection is heavily dependent upon institutional provision (for example, location and accessibility of services and programs), and institutional processes (for example, inclusive and participatory methods). Where young people are marginalised from the major social institutions, such as school, work, family, religion and recreation, then there is greater chance they will come to be seen as a threat to the order of a society which seems to have rejected them.

CITIZEN AND RESPONSIBILITY

One of the dimensions of livelihood—of 'belonging' in one's society and having the opportunity to contribute—is the exercise of rights to citizenship. Although citizenship is frequently mentioned with regard to young people in terms of young people's responsibilities, society also has a responsibilty to recognise young people as citizens.

The state plays a central role in youth development and livelihood. From the point of view of institutional analysis, the 'state' can be seen to comprise an expansive amalgam of various institutions, incorporating both elected and non-elected officials. For example, it may include the legislature (parliament), the public service (including social security), the judiciary and courts (state, federal), public order agencies (armed forces, police), utility companies (water, energy), regulatory bodies (broadcasting commission, industry boards), and public welfare agencies and institutions (hospitals, schools). From the point of view of broad social role, the 'state' is usually seen in terms of performing the function of facilitating and enhancing general economic activity, maintaining law and order, and ensuring the legitimacy of the social order generally. The issue of 'whose interests' the state represents in a liberal capitalist society is a matter of much contention. Reference to the 'welfare state' alludes to the fact that particularly during and immediately after the Second World War, many countries saw major changes whereby the state assumed greater responsibility for social wellbeing in areas such as education and health.

One of the transformations presently taking place in the nature of the welfare state is the transformation of the 'citizen' from being a 'rights holder' to that of 'responsible consumer'. Young people are centrally positioned in this transformation. To understand these changes it is essential to explore the distinction between citizens (that is, individuals with a relationship to the state) and class subjects (that is, citizens defined in relational and collective terms).

The idea of the liberal democratic state is premised on the notion of a 'social contract' between discrete individuals and the state. In this framework it is supposed that each person gives up certain rights to the state in return for the protection of property and person by the state. The extension of 'democracy' to include first, the newly emerging capitalist class, and then the working class, women, indigenous people and younger people (that is, from 21 years of age to those aged 18), promised that the state would for all intents and purposes be an organ and expression of the 'people'. That this did not, and has not, threatened the basic structures and inequalities of capitalism is one of the more intriguing points of political science. The combination of liberalism (that is, protection of individual rights) and democratic form (that is, periodic elections) has provided a strong cover for the reproduction of class division and class-related exploitation.

The advent of the 'welfare state' meant that the form of the modern nation-state took on the appearance of a benevolent and class-neutral body, the main purpose of which is to look after the interests of its 'citizens'. In part, the development of the welfare apparatus was the result of class conflict over social surplus, a struggle which ultimately led to a class compromise in many of the advanced capitalist countries. From the period of the Second World War until the mid-1970s the welfare apparatus was expanded to include all kinds of benefits to citizens, things such as public schooling, free tertiary education, health and sickness benefits and services, welfare and counselling systems, old age and disability pensions.

By the mid- to late 1970s a series of changes in policy, program orientation and fiscal priority had begun. The welfare state was now officially 'in crisis'. In most of the advanced industrial countries, especially those with highly developed welfare apparatus, the allocation of services and benefits became increasingly selective. This also had major implications with regard to youth policy and that resource allocation which specifically targeted young people (see, for example, Irving et al. 1995). Ideologically, the demise of the 'welfare state' was justified in terms of the transition from 'Keynesian economics' towards economic rationalism, with the latter coming to dominate government and bureaucratic circles as the new orthodoxy of economic planning and thinking. The emphasis was not on the 'citizen rights' of the social liberals, but the efficiency concerns of the economic liberals (Beilharz et al. 1992; Pusey 1993).

Responsibility for wellbeing has thus been shifted from the social to the individual. This marks the breakdown of the post-war social democratic settlement, the ascendancy of economic rationalism as a practical ideology, and the reaffirmation of classical capitalist tenets vis-à-vis working class health and welfare. Empirically it can be demonstrated that both capital and the state are placing the onus of responsibility on the backs of individuals, even though the social problems and fiscal processes are structural in nature.

The ideology of citizenship has shifted away from the rights of the citizen to universal social supports, as well as basic protections provided by the state. In its stead, there is the view that citizens are best portrayed as 'consumers' of social services, and that the role of the state is but to facilitate this consumption, preferably via the use of private providers. Accompanying this view, greater emphasis has been placed on the 'responsibilities' of citizens to maintain their neighbourhoods, to pay for their own education and health, and to participate in their own crime prevention and security arrangements. The movement from 'welfare' state to 'repressive' state involves a retreat from developmental service provision and a greater fixation with the coercive apparatus and policing role of the state (see White 1996). Again, this has had enormous implications for how the state has responded to those young people who have not been able to 'consume' the right way, to 'be responsible' in the appropriate manner and to accept their duty as citizens to ensure the maintenance of good order in the society at large.

From the point of view of class analysis and the economic position of young people, there are a number of disturbing trends which affect their present situation and their future livelihoods. For example, the status of young people as bona fide citizens has been seriously eroded by the de-legitimation of 'rights' discourse generally, and by the impact of measures chosen to deal with the fiscal crises of the state. In particular, changes in criminal justice towards the so called 'justice' approach (rather than the previous model of 'welfare' approaches) signalled the turn towards personal, individual responsibility for one's actions, regardless of wider social context. This is reflected in numerous other ways as well, such as in 'case management' types of welfare intervention, the rejuvenation of 'measurable individual differences' as a guiding philosophy behind school testing, and the constant media barrage which sees 'difference' entirely in terms of the 'unique' individual.

At an institutional level, and as will be explored in greater depth in chapter six, the combination of welfare cuts and increased policing of street-present young people has fed a dangerous and growing concern with 'law and order'. The marginalised in our societies are thus in the frontline of incredibly repressive state policies which are presented as being popular with the 'masses' but which hold the most threat to basic democratic principles and important human rights. How we deal with the young marginalised, and the conditions which generate their material circumstances and behaviour, is symptomatic of the dilemmas and issues which must be confronted as capitalism enters a new millennium.

CONCLUSION

This chapter has provided a broad survey of issues relating to young people and the economy. We argue for the centrality of class analysis in youth studies research. In essence, the relations and processes of class set the parameters or boundaries within which a wide range of personal and situational practices and activities may occur. It is the pressures of and limits set by capitalism which establish the contours of youth experience, and the diverse institutional and cultural processes associated with this experience. As we shall see, any concept of 'youth development' which does not link the personal, the individual, to these wider class realities will be severely limited in its explanatory power and scope. It is to these issues that we now turn.

3 Youth development

This chapter focuses on *youth development*, a framework for conceptualising youth which is embedded in social psychological theories of human development. The study of youth has inherited a powerful legacy from this approach which is written into many assumptions about young people and about what it means to 'grow up'. Most importantly, the notion of 'youth development' permeates and informs many practices in schools and in other institutions which concern themselves with young people, such as correctional institutions and welfare agencies. 'Youth development' is the conceptual edifice on which the practices which marginalise some young people are based. Without the highly individualised notion of 'youth development' there would be no legitimation for the institutionalisation of discrimination through the mainstream curriculum, and the identification of young people who are 'at risk'.

It is especially relevant to subject the concept of youth development to critical attention now, because it has achieved a startling rebirth in the 1990s, serving as the rationale for regressive, judgemental and discriminatory practices in education and in the youth sector more broadly. These include the targeting of 'at risk' youth, standardised testing and the provision of resources for 'talented' or 'gifted' programs for selected youth, all of which are systematic institutional practices which serve to deny the significance of social divisions on young people's lives. The concept of youth development provides a rationale for the notion of a mainstream, a majority of around 80 to 90 per cent, who are on the same footing. The young people who do not conform to the standards of this mainstream are identified as those at risk, requiring specific attention to bring them into line with the mainstream.

Young people's relationship to schooling and their outcomes from schooling are integrally tied to relations of power: of class, gender, ethnicity and race. We cannot understand the outcomes of schooling as simply the result of individual characteristics such as ability, intellectual capacity, intelligence or appearance. Inequalities in outcomes are not just the concern of the poor, of young women or of young black people—they are the *effects* of a systematic pattern of relationships involving the school as a whole. The consistent finding that young people from poor families in Australia do not complete secondary schooling to the same extent as those from higher socio-economic backgrounds (Batten & Russell 1995) is not evidence of individual failure, but the worst effects of a *larger pattern* in which some are also exceptionally advantaged (Connell 1994).

In the following sections we firstly discuss the concept of adolescence, the cornerstone of the developmental model of youth. We offer a critique of this concept, based on the emerging evidence from research, which questions the link between physical and social 'maturation'. The concept of adolescence defines young people primarily in terms of inherent biological and psychological processes. Youth development approaches take this concept as the starting point of analysis of young people. The social world is an 'influence' on these fundamental processes, but is seen as very much a secondary consideration.

Following our discussion of the concept of adolescence, the next sections on gender and race provide examples of the limitations of the youth development approach to understanding young people. We then turn to two of the most frequently used concepts which draw on the youth development approach: *individual difference* and *risk-taking*. Both of these ideas continue to be influential in the practices of institutions such as schools and correctional institutions; they deserve greater scrutiny.

ADOLESCENCE (DEFINING THE 'GOOD', THE 'BAD' AND THE 'UGLY')

The concept of adolescence is integral to the youth development approach to conceptualising youth—it is the cornerstone. 'Adolescence' is the term which refers to a series of developmental stages involving mental and physical and psychological maturing that, it is assumed, all people go through. The adolescent stage of development is generally identified as the 'teenage years', although in the recent literature on adolescence, advocates are reluctant to correlate an exact age with the process (see Heaven 1994). Key elements of this approach are summarised in the following extract from Klein:

> Adolescence, using current conceptualisations, is characterised by the individual's attempt to develop a world outlook which will carry him or her through life, and guide his or her experiences accordingly. It is a time of experimentation—of 'trying on' new roles to determine which ones 'fit,' and rejecting those that do not. Adolescence is a time of emotional and financial dependency upon one's family-of-origin, yet, simultaneously, a time of rebellious social independence from the family unit. Among the many tasks to complete during adolescence are sexual identity formation, making preliminary career decisions, and beginning to take responsibility for one's actions. Adolescence, as now conceived, is a time in which people are granted some leeway in making errors, as long as those mistakes are part of the growing up process. Thus, irresponsibility and 'youthful recklessness' are still tolerated and rationalised away as simply being part of the adolescent phase of development (1990, pp. 459–60).

Central to this conceptualisation of youth is the idea that there are clearly identifiable processes which are universal. By definition, all normal young people must go through these set stages, completing their developmental tasks, in order to have any chance of being 'normal' adults. Adolescence, as a stage of mental and physical development is seen as so all-encompassing that the young people are referred to as 'adolescents'. Another central assumption of this perspective is the idea that this is a dangerous time (traditionally referred to as a time of 'storm and stress') in which individuals make rational choices about their future identity, 'trying on' a number of personae before finding their appropriate place in the social order. Although it is not necessarily assumed that all individuals make their choices from roughly the same social location, with roughly the same resources and goals, the emphasis on the psychological processes occurring within the individual make it difficult for this perspective to acknowledge social as well as psychological processes.

The concept of adolescence basically assumes a 'pre-social' self (Johnson 1993), which exists within the individual but which must be found and developed ('finding one's self'). The individual is seen as distinct from and separate from society, as possessing a 'self' independent from social relationships or social circumstances. This aspect of the concept of adolescence is important to the idea that something very distinct is happening at this stage, because once the 'self' is found, then it is established for life (see table 1.1). Hence, this dimension of adolescence is central to the view that 'adolescence' is very distinct from adult life. It is built on the assumption that life-long change and development which continue to influence one's identity do not occur. The widespread acceptance of this assumption may account for the way in which many women assume that, because they experience changes in their identity throughout life, associated with changes in their life circumstances such as the separation from a partner, the establishment of a career, or the independence of their children, they are not sure when they have become 'adult' (Greer 1991). Although 'growing up' does involve the establishment of an identity, this is not necessarily 'fixed' and may go through significant change during one's life.

A further implication of the separation of the individual from the social is that young people are positioned as vulnerable (at risk) because a number of influences may occur which irreparably damage the process of growing up as 'normal'. For example, belonging to a single-parent family has been identified in the past as a 'risk factor' for adolescents, as has the 'peer group'. These are 'risk factors' because they place the young person 'at risk' in the process of establishing their identity.

In addition, this perspective also identifies areas in which deficiencies in the young person's life (for example, their socioeconomic background) are associated with failure to adequately develop in a number of areas. It is the task of adolescence to reach the appropriate level of development in relation to each of these areas. They are identified by Heaven (1994) as the following: identity formation, social relationships (family and peer group), education, sexuality, parenthood (teenage parents), work and money—all the most fundamental aspects of not only young people's, but everybody's lives, in fact. It is assumed that young people can 'fail' to achieve the correct level of development in each of these areas (for which there are yardsticks of success), and without professional attention and intervention will be at risk of remaining incomplete. In addition, Heaven discusses the 'problem areas' identified with youth, of delinquency in relation to authority, depression and suicide. The study of adolescence is dominated by a focus on those who have failed to become normal, and hence are defined as a problem. The problem is located either in the *individual,* as a deficiency, or with *family relations,* which are seen in terms of social pathology (illness).

This approach has been especially significant in educational institutions as a basis for ordering and legitimating success and failure as an individual characteristic, and as a legitimation for the involvement of professionals in young people's lives. Griffin, for example, provides a detailed critique of the developmental model for both Britain and the United States. She comments that the 'ideological legacy' of this construction of youth is 'still evident in the force of the clinical and psychological focus on individual young people as potential problems, and the representation of adolescence as an age

stage which will inevitably involve forms of psychological distur-
bance' (1993, p. 160).

The focus on individual characteristics, the problematising of
youth as an age group, and their categorisation into a single entity
differentiated only by 'normal' (or 'mainstream') and 'deviant' (or
'at risk'), contrasts markedly with the perspectives young people
themselves have about youth. Young people are seldom heard to
refer to each other as adolescents. From their own perspectives some
young people are seen to be like themselves, but they can see that
most are not. Almost all ethnographic studies of young people reveal
an acute awareness of difference amongst young people. Denholm
(1993) provides a useful description of the ways in which young
people in the Australian state of Tasmania differentiate each other
on the basis of style. Davies' girls and boys from three schools in
New South Wales also constantly referred to the ways in which they
were different from other groups. Her descriptions of the talk of the
girls from St Clements (a private, elite school) clearly illustrates their
awareness of themselves as different from the girls—and the boys—
who go to the public schools through their adherence to different
codes of feminine behaviour (Davies 1993). They noted differences
in speech, dress and behaviour as central. Their identity is integrally
related to their ability to negotiate the meanings that class and gender
have in their own context.

Wexler's young people in three schools in the United States show
the same acute awareness of difference and of relations of power.
His ethnographic study of young people and their negotiation and
construction of identity reveals how the experience and the meaning
of everyday life is different. Wexler argues that, 'the ideal and the
route to becoming somebody in the *suburban white working class*
is not the same as becoming somebody in a high school in a
professional middle class suburb' (Wexler 1992, p. 8). His students
were also aware of the extent to which they become defined as a
problem and classified as an object for attention by professionals.
When Wexler interviewed students from one of the poorest schools,
they asked him not to perpetuate the reputation that their school
was not a good place:

> Student: I want it to be classified like any normal school. Our skills
> and our academic work might not be classified as high as some sub-
> urban schools *but we want it to be known that we are not bad*. But
> we want it to be known that we are friendly . . . We just have to
> show them—show them that we are good and not as they say . . .
> In my opinion it's a great place. You see a lot of different people of
> different backgrounds, not all rich and not all poor. Different back-

grounds, you know. Interesting and friendly people. (Wexler 1992, pp. 75–6).

The popularity of the term 'adolescent' is perpetuated not by young people themselves and not by those who take serious account of their perspectives and experiences. The use of the term 'adolescent' is a signal that the young people being referred to are being objectified, categorised and judged. This is most evident in the assumption that although the process of development is basically assumed to be 'natural', 'abnormal' development may occur if the circumstances are not right. In this way, developmental models of youth construct youth as vulnerable, and offer judgement about who is 'normal' and who is 'at risk'. In educational institutions especially, concern is frequently focused on the vulnerability of a minority of young people to educational failure. These are the 'at risk'.

A recent summary of British, US, Canadian and Australian literature on 'young people at risk' confirms that in each of these countries there is a high level of concern that a proportion of young people fail at school and are thereby disadvantaged in the competition to get jobs in the primary labour market of relatively secure and relatively well-paid jobs (Withers & Batten 1995). In 1990 Lubeck and Garrett (1990) estimated that fully one-third of all school-age children in the United States were at risk of academic failure. In Australia it has been estimated that one-sixth of young people aged between 15 and 19 are already marginalised through failure at school, and are in neither full-time education nor full-time work (Sweet 1992).

More recently, the 1993 report of the At-Risk Youth Task Force of the State Employment and Training Commission of the State of New Jersey (as quoted in Withers & Batten 1995) identified 'making it in the Global Economy' as the real challenge that faces young people. This report on 'at risk' youth provides a good example of the way in which structured inequality becomes identified as an individual problem. This report suggests that two related phenomena are responsible for placing young people at risk of failure: families do not give young people enough support, and higher educational levels are required for entry into the labour market (Withers & Batten 1995, p. 6).

Having identified individual families and levels of educational attainment as remiss, this report, like many of the others quoted in this collection, suggests a list of skills or 'competencies' which young people need to have in order to be successful. In other words, the solution to the structural problem of the labour market is firmly located in individual performance and attainment. Young people (and their families) are seen as 'the problem', the solution to which is to remedy the deficiencies in their attainment and performance. The concept of young people 'at risk' defines the nature of the social problem of failure in a particular way. Young people who are 'at risk' are those who are or will be unable to use the opportunities that school presents. 'The problem of poor school performance resides not in social, political, economic, and educational institution, but rather in the child, and, by extension, in the family' (Lubeck & Garrett 1990, p. 327).

The legacy of the concept of adolescence lies also in the dominance of a biologically determinist approach to the processes of growing up. This approach allows educational experts to take elaborate measures in the supposed interests of young people who are at risk of failure, while ignoring the 'mystery in broad daylight' to which Connell refers: poor people are the least successful in education and what students in poverty experience in school is lack of power (Connell 1994, p. 133). Instead, 'the human condition is conceived of as a continuum, in which all that is normative is considered positive. Anyone experiencing anything unexpected or unpleasant is potentially at risk' (Lubeck & Garrett 1990, p. 328).

A recent Australian study of educational outcomes sought to measure the levels of equity in the outcomes of schooling for different groups of young people, based on labour force regions, as a reflection of socioeconomic background (Teese et al. 1993). The report reveals that social class and gender are the most reliable predictors of success and failure at school, of the likelihood of succeeding in particular subjects and of the likelihood of taking up tertiary study. For example, young people living in a working class region, whose parents' occupations were in the professional category were twice as likely as their local peers whose parents' occupations were in the blue collar category to obtain honours at the chemistry exams. However, young people whose parents' occupation were in the professional category and who lived in a middle class region were more than three times as likely as the most typical student in the working class region to achieve honours in this subject. The pattern is repeated for all subjects. As a consequence of these unequal outcomes, the lower the social status, the less likely a young person will be offered a place in higher education.

Standardised testing, which places each individual in competition with all others is based on the rationale that all individuals are on the same footing. As Teese et al. comment, the wide group-based differences in educational outcomes are regularly masked by tests that simply measure random individual outcomes (for example, comparing the results in English at the end of primary school). The legacy of the youth development model remains in the unwillingness of educational institutions to explore, measure and monitor social outcomes, on a regional or community basis. In effect, Teese et al. argue, the education system itself has 'crystallised around the strengths of its strongest users and become rigid and resistant to the needs of the weakest and most vulnerable' (1993, p. 1). Furthermore, the 'strongest' users of this system (those who are offered success) are the children of professionals and boys, and the 'weakest' (those who are less successful, and those who fail) are the children of unemployed and unskilled workers. The ideology of 'measurable individual difference' which underpins the use of standardised testing is found wanting when class, gender and ethnicity are taken into account in the actual outcomes for young people.

The limitations of the youth development model are discussed over the following pages in more detail. We first discuss the conceptualisation of gender within this framework, then take up issues of 'race'. In both of these areas, the youth development approach provides a biological determinist model of development, emphasising the assumed 'naturalness' of behaviours and characteristics associated with femininity, masculinity and with particular ethnic groups. Recent research on gender and race illustrates the serious limitations of the youth development approach.

GENDER AND DEVELOPMENT

There are two fundamental limitations to the youth development approach which are illustrated by research and writing on gender and youth. Firstly, the stages of development which are set within this perspective are wrong for women. The idea of linear development towards the fully autonomous, independent individual can only be seen to 'fit' women's experiences of growing up if many aspects of women's experience are ignored. Secondly, even if the stages were to be redefined, or added to, to incorporate feminine as well as masculine experiences of growing up, the assumption that this process is essentially an individual and ahistorical process, and that there can be a universal model for particular groups and that it is a linear process, is flawed.

Recently a number of youth researchers have explored the developmental approach to understanding the experience of growing up for women. We have already referred to the work of Johnson (1993), who has provided an analysis of the developmental psychological approach in relation to women and education in Australia in the 1950s. Her study offers a useful insight into the development of an industry (of developmental psychology) based on monitoring young people to assist them in the task of becoming adult.

Johnson argues that what emerged in the 1950s was the increasing involvement of professionals in the creation of the 'modern personality' as a self-determining identity, which involved the resolution of a struggle between the needs of individuals and those of society. The 'ideal of the autonomous personality' or the 'pre-social self' central to the concept of adolescence was the individual seeking independence, defining the self separately from social relationships (Johnson 1993, p. 66), and defining the social as separate from the individual. Hence, the developmental task for young women in the 1950s was to find their 'true' identity by 'naturally' choosing to become wives and mothers. Young women were assisted in this developmental task by an education system which asked girls to think of themselves first and foremost as sexed identities.

Through an analysis of the media of the day, Johnson identifies examples of what the 'sexed identities' were to be. For example, she quotes an item in a Sydney newspaper of 1953 which reports on a high school fashion parade, in which school girls paraded the clothes they had made at school. The item includes the following:

> Classrooms were transformed into dressing rooms for the parade, and when the girls emerged in the school corridors in their pretty dresses, high-heeled shoes and lipstick—instead of the baggy tunic— teachers commented, 'Well they all look at least three years older!' (quoted in Johnson 1993 p. 79).

These young women were learning to produce themselves in the appropriate feminine form, a 'feminised bodily existence in "pretty clothes" and of "mature" appearance' (Johnson 1993, p. 79). Publicly drawing attention to how the young women looked served to underline that these young women were not just parading the clothes they had made—they were parading their new 'selves'. In the framework of developmental psychology, this behaviour is seen as part of the 'natural' process of 'trying on' different selves before settling on the right one. However, a sociological analysis would point out the strength of social pressure for these young women to make a particular 'choice'. Johnson's work reveals the way in which the ideology of youth development was central in the systematic production of sexed identities through the processes of schooling in the 1950s. Her work also clearly illustrates the historically specific nature of growing up. Young Australian women in the 1950s were engaging with a very different set of conditions in negotiating the process of growing up from those being negotiated by young women in the 1990s. Yet, despite the historical differences, Johnson argues that what women are likely to experience in common is that there is not a clear developmental path with set stages along the way marking departures and arrivals in status.

Her work confirms that the developmental psychological approach to youth development is based on masculine experience. The universal 'human experience' that is defined in the developmental model refers to the options, experiences, struggles and outcomes most common to some groups of men. One of the complexities of the universal developmental model is woven around the notion that the normal developmental process involves a linear progression from dependence to independence. The very notion of 'independence' is tied to a particular representation of male experience. Approaching this issue from a different angle, Gilligan (1982) has also suggested that the model of development that psychologists have traditionally used is inadequate for understanding women's experience. She suggests that women are more likely to seek and develop 'connectedness' and relationships with others—to develop *interdependence*—rather than 'independence'. Johnson describes the tangled line of argument produced within traditional developmental psychology during the 1950s to deal with women's experience. She describes Havinghurst's argument that girls have to become autonomous, self-defining individuals just as boys do, but that girls achieve this by learning that their role is to be economically dependent on a man (Johnson 1993, p. 65).

Griffin (1993) explores the literature on youth development from Britain and the United States. She argues that the concept of adolescence is both sexualised and criminalised. She points to the extent of concern about monitoring and judging young women's sexuality which tends to focus on teenage pregnancy, teenage motherhood and adolescent female sexuality. Griffin also argues that the concept of adolescence is criminalised, especially for young men, young people who are working class, and young people of 'race' and colour.

One of the issues that Griffin focuses on is the way in which developmental psychology assumes that 'normal' development must mean becoming heterosexual. She argues that in Britain and in the United States, there have been regular 'moral panics' over the fear that the transition to 'normal' heterosexual sexuality and nuclear family life may have been disrupted. She argues that within the discourse of development, all young people are presumed to be heterosexual; homosexuality is deviance from the norm. As she points out, sexuality is conflated with penetration (that is, penis–vagina), and penetration is elevated to a central initiation in adult life. As in other areas of life, the discourse of development constructs adolescent sexuality as a force which must be guided and controlled by experts, so that young people are able to make the transition into mature, heterosexual adults. Teenage pregnancy and motherhood are seen as evidence of a failure by young women to take the correct developmental path towards adulthood.

Most importantly, the use of the developmental model offers no grasp at all on the construction of gendered identities in which power relations are central. The overwhelming significance given to the individual, and the separation of individual from society perpetuates the notion that masculinities and femininities are simply complementary 'roles' which are taken up. Recent research on the construction of gendered identities and of sexuality reveals that power relations are a fundamental dimension. Masculinities and femininities are constructed in relation to each other.

An example is provided by research on young women's sexuality, in which one of the authors has been involved. In exploring the responses of young women to safer sex campaigns, it was found that even when young women were well informed about safer sexual practices, many were loath to put their knowledge into practice. They feared that to appear to know about sexuality would brand them, in the eyes of their partner, as a 'slut'. 'Good' women were ignorant, inexperienced and responsive but did not take the initiative in relation to their men, who should be more knowledgeable, experienced and able to take charge (Wyn 1994). The result of these perceptions by young women was often their acceptance of unsafe sexual practices. These understandings form an integral part of the negotiation of sexuality, and of gendered identity. To see the acceptance of unsafe sexual practices as simply 'risk-taking'—a characteristic of adolescence—is to explain away a fundamental aspect of the negotiation of power relations between young men and young women.

The concept of hegemonic masculinity has been widely used to grasp the relational nature of gender. Hegemonic masculinity is constructed in relation to other subordinated masculinities as well as in relation to women (Connell 1995). This framework for understanding gender relations is based on the understanding that there is a dominant masculinity which prescribes particular behaviour as normal and devalues other forms of behaviour. The idealised 'masculinity' is often built on contempt for women and gays and lesbians, and emphasises success in terms of wealth, power and status. In practice, being a man may involve a range of strategies designed to shape the behaviour of others in accordance with the idea. Some of these behaviours actually parallel those of the criminal justice system, as young men constantly police the behaviour of young women, both in terms of sex and sexuality and more broadly in terms of 'acceptable' feminine behaviours (Nava 1984). Hegemonic masculinity is dependent on and implicated in the enforcement of particular masculine and particular feminine behaviours. The youth development model misses the point of this entirely.

'RACE' AND DEVELOPMENT

We use the term 'race' here to refer to the social divisions which are based on perceptions of colour and on understandings about culture. The youth development approach has been shown to be especially limited in understanding the experiences of young people who are of colour, indigenous or other than the dominant language (e.g. English) background. In common with the research on gender, the two related issues of universality and of individuality arise. The processes of growing up, the construction of identity and the perspectives on adult life which young people bring are far from universal. This is especially well illustrated by the experiences and processes of young people from indigenous communities. Secondly, it is important to recognise the extent to which young people growing up in different communities in various ways construct their identity, not as an individual, but as part of a wider reality, which for some may also include a relationship with the physical environment.

Palmer and Collard (1993) for example, have taken issue with traditional perspectives on young Australian Aboriginal people. The young people in their research came to adulthood through a long process of learning the extent, form, and the formal rules and sanctions surrounding their connectedness to others and to their land. Becoming adult in their experience is not a linear move towards independence, in which getting a job can be seen as a significant marker of adult status. Getting a job is useful, but their 'adulthood', their adult identity, is not defined by employment to the same extent as for their non-Aboriginal counterparts. For these young people, the process of being adult much more reflects Johnson's (1993) description of an ongoing process, where there is an increased awareness of complexity, rather than the series of set stages defined within developmental approaches.

Commenting on the way in which youth studies in Australia has tended to conceptualise young Aboriginal people, Palmer and Collard are critical of the assumption that all young Aboriginal people are the same. They point out that young Aboriginal people are likely to have different attitudes and to have different experiences which divide them from each other. Palmer and Collard based their discussion on their research on the young Nyungar people, who were living in the southern metropolitan region of Perth. Their work produces a perspective on young Aboriginal people that challenges the view that they are powerless victims, mainly remote dwellers, and adolescents with more than the usual problems. Palmer and Collard argue that these are myths about young Aboriginal people which have been generated and perpetuated, although not exclusively through the youth development approach.

In addition, Palmer and Collard argue, the assumption that young people are 'individuals' is unhelpful in understanding their lives:

> By and large practitioners and policy makers tend to deal with Nyungar young people outside of their community and family context. The theme that 'youth' is a distinct, separable and identifiable period in human life is central to much of the thinking in youth studies . . . In contrast the Nyungar people often see the lives and welfare of their young people as intricately tied up with the family or community expectations and responsibilities rather than as a distant and separate issue (Palmer & Collard 1993, p. 118).

In the Canadian context, Webster and Nabigon's discussion of the perspectives of first nations communities also underlines the inappropriateness of the youth development model. Webster and Nabigon (1993) point out that first nations people are heterogeneous, undermining the value of portrayals of a 'collective Indian personality'. 'Cultural investigations have identified numerous family types including traditional, transitional, bicultural, and pan-traditional', which do not measure 'Indianness', but rather, different transactional styles among Indian families. The authors also suggest that the use of traditional (psychological) measures of self-concept are inappropriate. Traditional measures invariably produce the finding that Indian people have a poor self-concept. Webster and Nabigon (1993) describe a study of Indian self-concept which made use of native interpretations and meanings of attitudes towards the self, and which concluded that this method is more likely to produce the finding that Indian people have a moderately positive self-concept.

This research leads to the conclusion that it is important to have an understanding of the experiences different groups of young people have of growing up that draws on their perspectives. The youth development model imposes a highly ethnocentric and masculine model of human development which does ultimately reveal more about the practices of professionals and experts than it does about the young people whose lives it is intended to address.

The assumptions underlying the youth development model have been especially detrimental to young people of colour and some from non-English-speaking backgrounds. In educational circles, the term 'multicultural' has been used to refer to educational practices which take into account the social differences which systematically mark young people from different cultural backgrounds. Yet, the use of standardised tests to measure educational achievement brings into the foreground practices which assume that educational achievement is a universal and innate characteristic that can be measured 'objectively'.

Standardised tests of educational attainment, like those which purport to measure IQ, are given credibility because they are said to be constructed in such a way that they exclude 'outside influences'. They are assumed to measure only 'inside' capacities or characteristics. However, as Demaine (1989) comments in his discussion of the categorisation of race and educational achievement in Britain, it is precisely this notion of outside/inside which is untenable. The very concept of innate intellectual potential, severed from the social relationships that constitute individuals, is at the heart of the youth development approach, in which the individual is seen as separate from society, possessing individual capacities, or deficits.

In a study of three schools in the United States, Wexler (1992) comments that the majority of the students at the poorest school were African and Hispanic youths, who experienced systematic conflict with the school's teachers and administration. Wexler argues that 'the school is not racist', but that nonetheless the school systematically discriminated against students on the basis of race. The teachers generally accepted the school's classification system, based on testing, and saw individuals in the light of 'the failure syndrome' traced back to family 'deficits' (Wexler 1992, p. 125). He adds that neither the idea of deficit in this context nor the school's classification system were explored in relation to questions of opportunity, class and race. Instead, at this school, many students are 'systematically categorised as handicapped or incapacitated on cognitive, emotional or behavioral dimensions' (Wexler 1992, p. 124).

The impact of failure, of the negative judgements made about young people which inevitably follows from the youth development approach, is to marginalise particular groups of young people. In Wexler's study, the students were aware that race was an issue, and that the categorisation was linked to a depth of moral approval and opprobrium. This awareness is also apparent in the views of students in Australian schools in the study by Connell et al. (1982). In this study, the processes of categorisation which are involved in establishing hierarchical social institutions are seen to systematically marginalise young working class people, many of whom are of non-English speaking background.

INDIVIDUAL DIFFERENCE AND SOCIAL PRACTICES

Of course all young people are different from each other. Even within families where, arguably, the same social conditions are present, people sometimes seem to grow up to be different from each other in quite fundamental ways. The idea of individual difference is given primacy within the notion of youth development because it is assumed that development is overwhelmingly an individual process. Although social or 'external' factors are acknowledged, these are simply seen as interventions (usually detrimental) rather than integral in the process of developing identity and growing up. Some of the implications of giving primacy to individual difference have already been discussed above. The separation of the individual from society, for example, has been criticised for its inappropriateness to the task of understanding the experiences of girls as they negotiate womanhood, and the experiences of young people from indigenous communities. The research on these groups helps to reveal the profoundly social nature of the 'individual'. We explore this point further by exploring the social nature of identity as a central dimension of the individual.

We turn once again to the implications of the false splitting of the *individual* and *social* that is inherent in the notion of individual difference. Although the youth development model provides a perspective on the extent of individual difference, the results of this are a denial of the validity of the full spectrum of young people's capacities, perspectives and identities. The youth development approach offers institutions such as schools (and families) a discourse within which some attributes, characteristics or 'gifts' are given more recognition, value and greater resources, and others are devalued, ignored or pathologised.

Although each person is different and unique in some way, people construct their identities through social interaction. It is this process that Wexler (1992) calls 'becoming somebody', arguably the most important and consuming activity of young people, and for many adults as well. One of the key places where this happens is in schools, because these are places where people are 'engaged with each other in the interactional work of making *meaning*. These are places for making the CORE meaning, of self or identity among people' (Wexler 1992, p. 155). Producing meaning is structured and organised in schools, as it is in families and other institutions.

To turn to an Australian example, Diamond's (1991) discussion of Tanya provides a useful illustration of the negotiation of identity, and the way in which social practices operate. Tanya was working very hard on becoming 'somebody' in her school. According to Diamond, she put much more effort into developing her social competence as a 'citizen' than on her formal school work. Mainly, she practised challenging the teachers' control, and by her second year at school had become known as a troublemaker, bringing her parents into the struggle to create a more submissive individual. Tanya's attempt to have control over how she represented herself (as a young woman and as an individual) were not very successful. The powerful discourse of youth development which the teachers made use of served to construct her as 'an individual without reason and deficient in terms of the responsibility which results from an acceptance of the school's definition of individual choice' (Diamond 1991, p. 155). The school gave her the opportunity to 'choose' to be someone she was not. She rejected this 'choice', but, at least in the short term, suffered the consequences of being judged negatively by her teachers, her parents and ultimately by her friends.

This type of negative outcome is the fundamental issue. Although youth development offers a perspective on individual difference, the discourse at the same time offers a highly judgemental approach and one which legitimates control over young people. Tanya was actively engaged in the work of developing her identity in the same way that Wexler describes the young people in the schools he studied were doing. Although young people are required to show responsibility for themselves within the school context, it is only allowed to be taken up in particular, limited ways. In the example offered by Tanya's experience, we can see how the school's concept of 'responsible' behaviour was gendered.

Identities are constructed within webs of meaning that are classed, gendered and 'raced'. Individual differences reflect the way in which particular individuals engage with the processes of class, gender, 'race' and ethnicity. What the individual difference *approach* fails to sufficiently acknowledge is that power relations are central. In the light of this, Tanya's 'discipline problem' can be seen instead as an attempt by a young woman to take power in a context where women are expected to be submissive. Penny, the young 'tomboy' in Davies' work (1989 and 1993) like Tanya, attempted to take a powerful position as a female. Ultimately, she too, at least in the short term, is constrained by the positioning of women as 'other' within the dualism of male–female.

Our discussion of gender and race has illustrated one of the most significant shortcomings of the youth development model. The emphasis on individual development, and on the power and accuracy of the theoretical developmental model, has been a central tool within education, welfare, social work and correctional institutions to support judgemental, discriminatory and invasive practices. The approach allows teachers, social workers and other professionals to place a positive value on some 'individual' characteristics and a negative value on others. The positive value associated with narrow academic achievement—institutionalised in 'gifted' programs for example—offers a clear value judgement that places some individual 'gifts' over and above others.

RISK-TAKING

'The psychosocial adjustment and mental health of adolescents are commonly recognised as factors in risk behaviour which can result in juvenile crime, substance abuse, homelessness, ill health and suicidal behaviour', according to a flier advertising a new book on Australia's adolescents. The idea of risky behaviour and of risk-taking is also central to the discourse of youth development. In place of the idea that adolescence is a time of 'storm and stress', the idea that young people take risks more than other groups of people remains very popular.

There are a number of assumptions involved in this notion that deserve greater scrutiny. Firstly, compared with which group are young people more 'risky'? The behaviours of the business magnates of the 1980s and 1990s would appear to have occurred within a culture of 'risk' which valued and encouraged systematically 'risky' behaviour and practices (using other people's money). Within the business community also, many employers are prepared to engage in behaviour and practices which place their employees at risk of injury and death, despite the existence of legislation to prohibit such practices (Perrone 1995). The focus on young people as inherently more prone to 'risky' behaviour is not borne out by this evidence.

The idea that young people are especially prone to take risks is linked with the concept of 'at risk' which is integral to youth development. The idea that young people are 'at risk' expresses the vulnerability of youth and childhood that is assumed within this approach. 'Innate defects in the child's nature, if left unchecked, would interact with equally dangerous elements in the social environment to produce disastrous consequences for the child and for society' (Miller et al. 1991). The very concept of adolescence implies that young people are 'at risk' and engaging in 'risky behaviours'. According to some, risk-taking can be measured in young people, as a personality trait (see Heaven 1994, p.198), which is associated with delinquency.

The usefulness of this approach is that it appears to give some control over young people or at least some predictability in relation to behaviour. Heaven cites studies on young people that are interpreted to show that 'extroverts' have a lower pain threshold than others: 'Accordingly, extroverts who are typically low on arousal are much more likely to engage in risky, thrill-enhancing behaviours. Many such behaviours are typical of delinquents and criminals' (Heaven 1994, p. 208).

Hence, risk-taking is seen to be linked with delinquent and criminal behaviour. The broader implications of linking the idea of 'extrovert' with criminal behaviour are that it may, in extreme cases, be linked with particular cultural groups who are assumed to put an emphasis on 'extroverted behaviour'. In Heaven's discussion, the idea of risk-taking is firmly tied to negative, unsocial and unacceptable behaviour. He claims that it is now believed that a single common factor accounts for problem behaviours in both young men and young women, and this is unconventionality in personality and social attributes (Heaven 1994, p. 202). From this perspective then, 'risk-taking' is a term that describes behaviour that is defined as unconventional by professionals. 'Risk behaviour' is a term that problematises certain behaviours.

There is another dimension to the idea of risk-taking that also needs to be explored. The very idea of risk implies a rational assessment of the chances of 'getting away with' something. Behaviour can only be described as 'risky' if it has been engaged in on the basis of a calculation of all the factors that might influence the outcome. The concept of risk-taking rests on an assumption of rationality.

For example, within criminology the focus of 'rational choice theory' is to modify the physical and social environment in order to reduce opportunities for crime. The basic premise of this approach is that all people, including young people, are responsible for their actions. However, it is thought that under given circumstances they will engage in offending behaviour if appropriate social controls are not in place to dissuade the making of the 'wrong choice'.

Research on young people's behaviour suggests that it is not necessarily appropriate to assume that 'rationality' (as narrowly conceived) is at work in young people's behaviour any more or less than it is for any other age group. Sexual practices provide a useful example. Young people's sexual lives have been a central focus in the youth development literature. As Griffin (1993) comments, research on 'adolescent sexuality' has operated within a discourse that focused on sexual deviance and on heterosexual initiation in an almost voyeuristic way. Within this discourse young people's practices are reduced to a concept of rational behaviour, in which relationships are seen as 'sexual experimentation' (assuming that one eventually finds the correct formula for sex, and so can end the 'experiment'). The idea of sexual risk-taking is central within this discourse.

Heterosexual practices have long held the 'risk' of pregnancy as an outcome. The last decade has brought the tragic effects of infection with HIV into the centre of discussion of sexual practices. In Australia (and to a lesser extent in Britain and the United States) it has been widely publicised through public campaigns and through formal educational strategies that some sexual practices, such as penetration without the protection of a condom carry a much higher risk of infection with the virus (and other sexually transmitted diseases) than other practices (such as wearing a condom or using non-penetrative practices). In the light of this public knowledge, there have been many studies which explore the extent of 'risky' sexual behaviour by young people. The research on young people's sexual behaviour appeared to reveal a paradox. Despite the extent of knowledge about the ways in which HIV is transmitted, and of the consequences of becoming infected with the virus, young people continued to have a relatively low use of safer sexual practices (Wyn 1994). This paradox became known in the literature as the 'knowledge–action gap'. Researchers whose approach drew on the discourse of youth development began to explain this phenomenon in terms of the natural tendency for young people to 'take risks'. Failure to use safer sexual practices was seen as an example of risky behaviour (for example, Rosenthal et al. 1994).

The paradox is explained if the perspectives of young people themselves are taken seriously. The educational campaign in Australia targeted women as the moral gatekeepers of sexuality, imploring them to 'tell him if it's not on, it's not on'. In other words, women were being asked to tell him 'no sex without a condom'. Although some young women were very comfortable with this idea, and could use it in practice, this suggestion placed many in a dilemma.

The discourses of masculinity and femininity operate powerfully, and not necessarily rationally at all. For many young women, admitting to being knowledgeable about sexuality (by carrying a condom at the ready) or even knowing enough about the implications of sexual practices to ask her partner to use a condom are to be positioned as a slut. Gender relations pose real barriers for some young women to the use of safer sexual practices in casual sex situations. In situations where there is a 'relationship' there are also barriers to safer sexual practices. The ideology of 'true love' involves trust between the partners, which for some is demonstrated by having enough 'trust' to not use a condom (Wyn 1994). This is not just apparent in the behaviour of young people.

The research by Kippax et al. (1990) reveals that the same dilemmas about trust and the meaning of safer sexual practices arise for older couples. Long-term monogamous relationships are deemed to be a form of safer sexual practice in which partners can 'trust' that there is no chance of infection. Kippax et al. identify through their research that the ideology of trust in relationships is more important than the reality of the practices. The 'knowledge–action gap' is explained by the centrality of gender relations.

In the area of sexuality, what may appear to be simply 'risk-taking' behaviour, a 'normal' part of adolescence which, according to some, 'unconventional' youth are more predisposed to, takes on a different appearance when gender relations are taken into account. In negotiating the complexities of gender power relations, especially in the tricky territory of sexuality, practices that seem 'risky' can be seen to be a logical and 'rational' outcome of the negotiation of relations of power.

A further dimension to understanding young people's seemingly 'risky' behaviour is the understanding that the individual does not possess a 'unitary self'. The idea that the individual develops a 'self' that is consistent, unitary and non-contradictory (and hence is able to operate rationally in terms of balancing the risks of behaviour) has been subjected to considerable criticism. If it is understood that:

> . . . the person is not simply the rational person invented through seventeenth century Enlightenment thought . . . But the person is much more than this rational mind in control of action and desire. Desire may stem from rational argument, but it also stems from the inscribed bodies and emotions of each person, from images and storylines, from the imbrication of ways of knowing in the metaphors and patterns through which we come to know. These ways of knowing are not necessarily able to be consciously articulated (Davies 1993, pp. 11–12).

Hence, although all people at times engage in behaviour that is risky, it is far too simplistic to characterise 'risky behaviour' as an inevitable part of growing up. Behaviours that are described as risky from the youth development perspective may be understood as the result of young people's negotiation of the complexities of gender, class, race and age relations. The results may appear to be risky, but for the young people themselves they are simply a conventional response to a complex situation. In the youth development approach, risky behaviour is a useful category for the contradictory behaviours young people engage in. These behaviours are a problem if it is assumed that the 'normal' individual possesses a unitary self, and that rationality will always prevail over desire.

CONCLUSION

In this chapter we have taken issue with the youth development approach to understanding young people. We have argued that this approach continues to exert a powerful influence on the institutions and professions which process young people. In particular, educational failure has been identified as a central concern which frames the youth development approach. Understanding the implications and legacy of the youth development approach is fundamental to rethinking the concept of youth, and to rethinking the relationship between institutions such as schools and young people.

In our discussion, we have emphasised how integral schools are to the processes of identity development, not because young people naturally 'mature' there, but because in schools young people do the work of negotiating gender, class, race and other divisions. As Connell (1994) comments, educational failure is not about individuals, it is about the way in which whole systems advantage some and disadvantage, or marginalise, others. The youth development approach is central to these processes of judging, monitoring and failing young people on the falsely constructed notion of individual capacity.

Wexler (1992) has gone as far as to say that the extent to which schools in the United States fail young people is a direct reflection of the failure and disintegration of public life. As long as the legacy of youth development continues to hold sway, it will be impossible to even conceptualise the public, social and cultural contribution that schools will make to young people's lives. Meanwhile, in the 1990s, we are witnessing large-scale educational reforms that assume education to be largely a technical process of information transmission. These reforms rest securely on the notion that individuals are 'pre-social', that human development is simply a matter of natural maturation, and that the minority who do not conform can be given remedial attention.

We would agree with Wexler, and would add that the discourse of youth development actually provides a legitimation for denying young people rights which are provided for adults. By individualising and essentialising young people, a highly judgemental approach can be justified, which ultimately marginalises those who are the least powerful in our society. It is to the conceptualisation of identity in relation to the processes of social division that we turn in the following discussions of cultural formation.

4   Youth subcultures

How young people experience the world involves a wide range of feelings, knowledge, perceptions and relationships. The aim of this chapter is to explore the subjective dispositions (for example, personal thoughts, emotions) and 'cultural' activities (for example, ways of interacting, speaking, dressing) of young people from the point of view of the relationship between material circumstances and available modes of identity construction. Who young people are— their position in the social world, and their own perceptions of their position—is always complex and complicated. The intention of the chapter is to unpack some of this complexity, in particular by examining different aspects of youth cultural life and how this is shaped by wider structural developments and social forces (such as changing economic circumstances).

By way of introduction we can say that ideas of 'culture' and 'youth subcultures' are neither simple nor uncontested. Indeed, it is apparent from the literature in this area that there are many different definitions of 'culture'—from a 'whole way of life' through to matters of 'style'—as well as many different expressions of cultural life. In a similar vein, we can also note that young people occupy a very complex cultural universe, and this has a multitude of expressions at the level of lived experiences and behaviour.

At least initially, 'culture' can be seen to refer to distinct patterns of life, and the ways in which social groups give expression to their social and material life experience (Williams 1977; Hall & Jefferson 1976; Taylor 1993). In other words, from birth, people are inserted into particular configurations of meanings which establish, for them, the context, values and ideas by which they understand and negotiate their social worlds and natural environments. How young people experience life is thus a communal cultural process, one forged in association with family, friends and significant others in their lives.

A basic theme of this chapter is that cultural formation is an active process which involves the participation of young people, and which marks out different relationships to the dominant ideologies and values of society. In discussing the processes of cultural formation and youth identity, the chapter argues that identity is constructed through both the consumption and production of culture. Cultural formation means much more than the more superficial aspects of 'style'. Social identity is negotiated in the context of family and social institutions. A major concern of the chapter therefore is to explore the nature, level and degree of connection young people have with particular cultural forms, and how these relate to wider social processes and institutions.

Another concern of the chapter is to chart out the ways in which 'human agency' is circumscribed by social structure. That is, we wish to indicate the many ways in which personal choices are subject to the constraints, and opportunities, provided by wider social institutions. The complexities and limitations of choice are bound up with both immediate interactions with one's peers and family, and the economic and social resources available to different groups of young people. While the cultural world of young people may incorporate incredible diversity and differences, nevertheless, there are a series of commonalities which link together different sets or categories of young people (and their families and communities); these include things such as the bonds of class, gender, ethnicity and race.

DIMENSIONS OF CULTURAL FORMATION

As a distinctive 'way of life', *culture* refers to specific patterns of social interaction and the expressive form of people's social and material life experiences. Analysis of cultural formation therefore means going beyond the concept of subculture which is the staple of much work done in youth studies. While subcultural analysis has led to many insights about young people, and highlighted the diversity that exists, there is nevertheless a tendency in such work to essentialise youth cultural formation—that is, to focus on superficial aspects of culture, such as style, and the difference between young people and adults, while ignoring the continuities which exist across age boundaries. Within the context of a broad definition of culture, however, it is still important to identify a series of interrelated and overlapping cultural elements, including youth subcultures.

There is within any society a continual process of national cultural formation. This refers to a process whereby 'an apparent consensus is established within a society about its own identity and goals, according to which people are encouraged to measure their own sense of belonging and personal fulfilment' (Dwyer et al. 1984, p. 31). The apparent consensus that is established is represented as the significant or *dominant culture*. Generally this dominant culture incorporates a wide range of ideological and cultural elements (for example, notions of 'mateship', the idea of the 'lucky country', language patterns) which together reinforce a particular type and sense of social order. The sharing of the dominant culture is part of a process in which a 'commonsense' view of the nature of society is presented as part of the taken-for-granted world.

The production of specific meanings and ideas is in turn linked to the efforts and activities of the most powerful groups and classes in society to shape conceptions of reality to reflect their interests. This is a complex process, involving the articulation of diverse symbols and ideas in such a fashion as to establish a dominant world view. This process of *cultural hegemony* is one which draws upon a wide range of traditions, institutions and customs in order to preserve and extend the wealth and power of the dominant forces in any society (see Gramsci 1971; Williams 1977). The extensive diffusion and pre-eminence given to specific ideas and values (via the mass media, the schools and other social institutions), especially around 'national' symbols and themes, is usually done in such a way as to ignore, downplay or distort particular working class, immigrant, indigenous and female cultural traditions and experiences. Thus, for example, a supposed personal identification with being 'Australian' ('American', 'British', 'Canadian', 'German', 'French', etc.) glosses over real material differences between social groups and classes at the same time as it influences the experience of these differences.

How one identifies with the significant culture is mediated by where one stands in relation to *specific cultures*. A person's identity as an 'Aussie', for instance, is shaped by factors such as ethnic background (for example, Anglo-Celtic, Italian, Vietnamese), class background and gender. Social acceptance at the immediate level of home, neighbourhood and work relationships is conditioned by how well we fit into the values and traditions of particular categories and groups of people.

The experiences of working class males and females, for example, have been linked to cultural elements such as solidarity within the workplace and the neighbourhood, the importance attached to 'lived knowledge' which unites ideas and practical skills, informality in social networks, and finding fulfilment in personal labour power capacities (Dwyer et al. 1984). Differences in the construction of 'masculinity' and 'femininity' are also often bound up with different life experiences associated with class background (Donaldson 1987; Willis 1977; Griffin 1985; Segal 1990; Connell 1995). The distinction between a culture of masculinity and a culture of femininity itself indicates markedly different experiences, social expectations and life chances for men and women.

Recognition of the existence of the individual as a social subject is essential to any discussion of *youth culture*. The notion of youth culture is premised upon a basic similarity in position and ideas and revolves centrally around age. If it is taken to refer to youth concerns and attitudes, the concept of youth culture takes on a descriptive and universalising character in much the same way as the notion of 'generation consciousness'. For example, we could say that a central aspect of youth culture is that 'all young people' share similar problems in 'growing up', such as coming to terms with sex and sexuality, or finding ways to express their autonomy. The similarities between young people are seen to stem from their presumed common responses to a situation where, in general, they have fewer financial commitments, greater 'leisure' time, are the targets of teenage pop music and commercial enterprises, have marginal social status, and are seen primarily as consumers rather than producers. Mass entertainment venues and distinctive public institutions catering for young people further suggest a common basis for youth culture.

The extent of similarity in position and circumstance, attitudes and social preferences, however, still leaves begging a number of important questions. For if youth culture allows us to describe some apparently common features of lifestyle, it does not explain why and how different categories of young people act differently from each other and the diverse experiences of what being a young person means in practice. More fundamentally, the idea of a youth culture is problematic insofar as it is seen to somehow exist over and above any difference associated with class, ethnicity and gender.

The material basis for cultural difference becomes more apparent when we initially consider the nature of specific *youth subcultures*. Here we can make a distinction between youth subcultures which are closely tied to family background, and those which express a particular distinctiveness based upon, but separate from, the cultural and economic positioning of one's family.

In the former case, different ways of life involving different conceptions of values, attitudes, beliefs and practices have their origins in particular *parent cultures*. Walker's (1987) discussion of male youth subcultures in Sydney, for instance, makes a strong link between family background and youth group activity. In particular, major differences were apparent between the 'Aussies' and the 'Greeks' in terms of preferred sport, established versus migrant status and relationships to one's family. The influence of family background in the formation of subcultural practices and attitudes was particularly evident with respect to each group's aspirations and expectations regarding paid work. The 'Aussies' tended not to expect their working lives to differ greatly from their parents, and were perceived to adopt a 'she'll be right' attitude to the possibility of unemployment. The 'Greeks' on the other hand had a stronger sense of how long-term possibilities are created by short-term personal sacrifice. They were keenly conscious of this because of their parents' experiences in migrating from Greece to work in factories and steel mills in Australia.

While these kinds of subcultures represent particular variations of 'parent cultures', other types of subcultures appear to represent a sharper break with 'conventional' family cultural patterns and traditions. For instance, the so called 'spectacular' youth subcultures appear to involve a dramatic deviation from the dominant styles of dress and conventional behaviour (see Hall & Jefferson 1976; Hebdige 1979; Frith 1986; Brake 1985; White 1993a; Moore 1994). The particular distinctiveness of groups such as the teddy boys, mods, rockers, skinheads, punks and others lies in their appearance, language, preferred activities and friendship networks. It has been argued that, given the structural and cultural restrictions placed upon the choices available to young working class men and women, both in terms of job opportunities and spare-time activities, attempts are often made at a subcultural level to 'magically' resolve the dilemmas facing them (see Brake 1985; McRobbie & Nava 1984; McRobbie 1991). This might be done through the construction of specific kinds of symbolic identity, which are both unique to the group yet constitute a central bond for each member.

Cultural formation is an active process, one which involves young people themselves choosing and deciding aspects of their own identity and future. This is discussed in greater depth below. For the moment, we wish to simply point out that while the identity and cultural experiences of young people are contingent upon specific situational and structural factors, most young people are by and large fairly conventional in their behaviour and attitudes, most of the time.

To put it differently, even if we acknowledge differences in how social identity is constructed by different categories of young people, the mainstream social institutions such as school, family, media and commercial business set parameters on the expression of these differences. The cultural 'choices' available to young people seldom confront or contradict the key aspects of the dominant culture which provides 'commonsense' answers to issues of class division, sexism and racism. Social identity tends to be constructed in the context of and in relation to the dominant ideological processes of society. The processes of hegemony are precisely those which link broad cultural processes with certain ideological influences, which under capitalism tend to sustain class division and a range of oppressive social practices. Thus, while cultural formation is grounded in certain material and social conditions, it is also implicated in a continual process of domination and subordination.

UNIVERSAL AND PARTICULARISTIC IMAGES

It is important to acknowledge the existence of cultural difference across and between identifiable social groups, and to substantiate the material basis for any cultural difference. Too often, however, the public or popular literature on youth culture and youth subcultures either ignores the issue of difference, or when it is considered, it is not explained in much more than descriptive terms.

For example, we commonly see in the mass media attempts to *universalise youth culture and youth experience*. This takes the form of emphasising particular conceptions of young people (for example, psychological definitions of 'the adolescent'), and applying labels which are meant to capture the life experiences of a whole generation (for example, the notion of the 'troubled teenager'). The idea of a homogenous *youth culture* which is distinct and exclusive has featured prominently since the Second World War in many news and media reports.

Generalisations have varied from era to era, stressing the negative or the positive things about young people as the period warrants. Thus, the early 1950s tended to be a time when 'youth' was equated with vitality, optimism and a world of discovery. By the later part of the 1950s popular conceptions focused on issues such as 'juvenile delinquency' (and its associated subcultural forms present in certain types of dress, dance and music styles). Later, the 1960s saw the construction of the 'generation gap', which severed the connection between young person and adult world, between ascribed social background and immediate experience. By the 1980s and into the 1990s commentators spoke of young people as 'victims' or as 'threat s', and generally the emphasis was on youth as a 'wasted resource' (see Irving et al. 1995). The notion of a 'generation X', similarly, has been used to describe a generation without any real features or definitive characteristics except lack of a real presence in the world.

The problem with these kinds of generalisations and universalising statements is twofold. Firstly, at an analytical level, they serve to trivialise and make abstract the lived practices of different categories of youth in a way which distorts the social differences and diversity of experience among young people. Put simply, they provide a picture of young people which is factually incorrect.

Secondly, at a political level, one-sided exaggeration feeds particular policy and electoral responses to 'youth issues'. Thus, for example, the 'law and order' debate has been fed for several years now by images of marauding juveniles, youth gangs, unbridled youth violence and the like. The impact of such images is felt in both an expanded 'fear of crime' (without necessarily a corresponding empirical basis for this fear), and in policing strategies and political campaigns designed to control and limit the activities of *young people as a whole* (see White & Alder 1994).

These homogenising and universalising images of youth can be contrasted with the concrete discussions of specific 'problem youth', which have long been the concern of social scientists. The history of youth studies is replete with case studies of (usually) male 'delinquent gangs' and student 'resisters'. In these instances, analysis and representation see youth in more *particularistic ways*. That is, there is a sense of profound difference between different categories or groups of young people (White 1990; Brake 1985).

One issue here, however, is that while heterogeneity in the youth population is acknowledged, it is often done so in ways which merely describe subcultural form and activity, rather than explaining them in terms of wider social divisions and social theories (see, for example, Denholm 1993; Moore 1994). Conversely, those abstractly theorising about youth subcultures or the differences between groups of young people can be accused of not being sensitive enough to the actual lived reality of these young people (see Blackman 1995). Clearly, ethnographic study (involving for example, observation, interviews and conceptual analysis) is needed if we are to understand adequately the nature of the cultural worlds of the young.

The visibility of and differences among young people (on the basis of class, gender, ethnicity, 'race') are crucial to understanding the construction of youth as a 'social problem'. There are differential hierarchies and labelling of specific youth 'cultures' and youth 'groups'. These are devised on the basis of descriptive criteria such as general class or ethnic composition of a group, the main sort of activity in which a group engages, and the type of dress and language adopted by the group. Furthermore, a distinction can be drawn between cultural elements pertaining to a wide layer of the youth population (for example, girls and the 'cultures of femininity', boys and the 'cultures of masculinity'), and the more specific and distinctive practices and styles associated with particular subgroupings within these broad population layers (for example, rap, graffiti 'bombers' or self-proclaimed lesbian groups).

For present purposes, it can be said that one of the major limitations of analysis which targets specific subcultures is that the focus very often stresses the *youth* dimensions of these subcultures, over and above other types of cultural connection, formation and process. Specifically, there is a tendency to analytically separate out 'youth' from their immediate *community positions* as members of particular class, gender, ethnic and 'race' communities. What gets emphasised is their unique characteristics as members of a particular category of youth (for example, punk, Rasta, hiphop, graffiti, street dancers, surfies, skegs, wogs, druggies). What gets under-emphasised or unacknowledged are the *continuities in culture* (for example, language, world view, dress, relationship to 'outside' institutions such as school, police and work) which transcend the generations.

The things which young people, and older people, have in common—their shared experiences of mainstream institutions and life opportunities, of racism, sexism, heterosexism and class division—can be obfuscated by attention on youth activity as both *subcultural* (and somehow unattached or distant from a 'parent culture') and *youthful* (and thus somehow exclusive to young people only). What needs to be done, therefore, is to frame analysis in such a way that it can at one and the same time deal with the specificity of particular groups/activities, while simultaneously locating these groups/activities within the context of wider family and community cultural relationships.

One recent attempt to provide a more sophisticated ethnographic account of youth cultural forms is provided by Blackman (1995). In this investigation of four pupil groups, all of whom are regarded by the school as belonging to the academic elite, Blackman attempts to develop a new model of interpretation of specific group practices, meanings, rituals, relations and communications. Thus, in moving from what is termed a 'local ethnography' to a 'general ethnography', the model attempts to chart out youth cultural activity across various dimensions. These dimensions of experience are conceptualised in terms of 'specialised positions' (that is, rules and forms of communication both within and outside the groups), 'social relations of the face' (that is, different types of interaction within and between groups, evident in ritual practices), 'specialised semiotic' (that is, rules which create and relay the main elements of style, such as dress, language and music) and 'signature' (that is, integrating the previous three aspects into a coherent picture).

In addition to arguing for the continuing importance of ethnography in youth studies research, Blackman makes the point that such analysis must be able to connect youth to the wider structures of class, gender and race. To do this, it is necessary to create a 'language of description' which can be used to describe the internal relations within youth cultural forms, the relations between these social forms, and their interrelations with wider social structures (Blackman 1995, pp. 22–3). The integration of these levels of analysis is illustrated in Blackman's observations regarding the 'new wave girls' becoming feminist:

> Female bodily experience became the communal responsibility of the group. This behaviour was presented as part of their rituals of integrity: close and intense group relations created a powerful social base for opposing and challenging the patriarchal stance of both the school hierarchy and male pupils. Sexuality is an area where male control over women is strongest and is exercised at the level of language: in naming, defining and denying speech to women/girls. The new wave girls' discourse is about the right to speak and to define, and about identifying and challenging male control of language.

Such research, and the theoretical concerns which inform its central components, has the potential to link the so called micro and macro levels of analysis in an explicit and systematic manner. Furthermore, as Taylor (1993) comments, how we do youth subculture research embodies important political aspects, and can be integral to developing practical strategies for social change. Thus, not only is an integrated analysis important from the point of view of understanding youth style groups and the like, but study of youth groupings allows us to identify those values, practices and elements of agency which contain the possibility for social change.

Nevertheless, by focusing primarily on youth subcultures, whether from a conservative or a more progressive political perspective, the danger is that we lose sight of the wider forces and processes at play in ongoing cultural formation. In addition, the material circumstances of collectivities (for example, income levels, employment chances, experience of oppressive and repressive structures) are certainly not youth-specific, and thus have relevance across age categories (Buchanan 1993; White 1994). Furthermore, case studies of specific groups/activities (such as the punks, street dancers, teddy boys, bodgies and widgies) which spotlight the spectacular and the unusual may directly or indirectly feed various 'moral panics' concerning these particular categories of young people (Cohen 1972). Insofar as analysis is centred on 'the group', rather than on issues of structure (such as class, gender and ethnic distributions of societal resources and power), then there is a tendency to portray and respond to the needs of young people in ways which suggest *they have or are 'the problem'*.

LIVED EXPERIENCES AND SOCIAL IDENTITY

As we saw in the previous chapter, discussions of youth development often end by positing certain select groups of young people as being 'at risk'. This raises the question of the relationship between self-concept (individual development) and group identity. For if we are to explain the creation of 'at risk' children and young people, then we need to know more about how these young people form ideas about themselves, how they connect up with other like-minded young people, and how both personal and group identity are actually structured. Further to this, we need to assess whether or not the so called 'at risk' young people define themselves culturally as being 'at risk', and why these particular young people are so labelled by experts and professionals in the youth affairs area.

Our main concern here is with the 'social self', rather than with 'personality'. Indeed, there is no such thing as the individual in the abstract: human beings, as individuals, are always historical subjects who exist in communities of fellow human beings. The subjectivity(ies) of individuals—their beliefs, values, emotions and desires—are at one and the same time manifestations of material processes and experiences as a 'gendered' subject, a 'class' subject, a 'race' subject and so on. The analytical task is to conceptualise the negotiation of identity in different social worlds.

It is our view that social identity is constructed in the context of a series of lived experiences pertaining, in the first instance, to locality, family and community resources. Where one lives and grows up (that is, the physical terrain and social amenities available) has a major influence on how one literally sees the world, as well as how we directly experience things around us. Climbing trees or negotiating car traffic, tramping through wilderness or queuing at the zoo, coping with searing heat or soaking in waves of monsoonal rain—all speak to quite different local conditions, climates and personal relationships to the natural and built-up environments. The *physicality* of environment is a large part of how we experience the world around us.

Family context plays a huge role in shaping our identities and where we fit in the overall social world. Unfortunately, this central aspect of human experience tends to be ignored in much subcultural analysis per se, and similarly much work on the family is seldom linked to youth studies. Yet, consideration of the family is crucial to the analysis of youth. Whether one grows up in a nuclear or extended form of family affects how we view kin relations and adult interaction. Life experiences associated with specific cultural norms, including clashes between dominant Western family models (for example, with an emphasis on child dependency and discipline, and

82

separation of the child/adult worlds) and other models (for example, indigenous people who emphasise childhood freedom and unity of child/adult activity and presence), serve to mould one's identity and group ties in particular ways. Ultimately, our primary networks and relationships are formed in intimate settings among *significant others* such as parents, family and community.

Further identity formation takes places in *social institutions*, such as the school, workplace, leisure and recreation activities (both spectator and participant). Children are born into a series of intimate relations over which they have little choice or control. This is the rule of biology and chance, which governs us all—we do not choose the cradle. However, beyond the family domain there exists an institutionalised realm of social participation which is contingent, changing and historically constructed. This is where the 'at risk' child is constructed, where life performance is gauged, measured, labelled and assessed.

The sense of belonging is integral to social identity. The social institutions are also where young people develop ideas about their 'public' selves which tells them who they are. Identity is first and foremost about social connection. And this in turn is shaped by experiences within the social institutions.

CULTURAL LIFE AND SOCIAL PRACTICES

Our view of cultural life is premised on the idea that social being, as initially grounded in family life, sets the limits of and the pressures on social consciousness. That is, the *objective positioning* of people in the social world (their ascribed positions in terms of class, gender, ethnicity; their experiential position in terms of their exposure to media, music, films, videos) influences their *subjective positioning* in that world (group subcultures, personal identity formation). To put it differently, it is the 'external' material conditions which provide the broad canvas upon which is mapped one's self-identified attachments and belongings.

In more specific terms, it needs to be acknowledged that there are particular spheres or regions of group membership—the school, the street, leisure, music, dance—and young people have transient, and multiple memberships of groups in each of these kinds of spheres. *Social connection* is produced through a combination of pre-defined settings and situations (for example, classroom rules and compulsory schooling) and the relationships forged under these institutionalised circumstances (for example, between student and teacher and other students).

It is also reinforced in specific instances by overt, visible ٻ‚ٻ shared experience or styles of relating to the world. For example, the adoption of particular kinds of language, dress, attitudes, posture and image all provide indicators of distance from or proximity to different forms of cultural being (such as acceptance or rejection of the school's educational and disciplinary regime). Ultimately, the relationship young people have with specific institutional cultures (such as the school regime) has a bearing on where they stand, materially and culturally, in relation to the general hegemonic processes of cultural domination (that is, the ideologies and practices which justify unequal distribution of societal resources and oppressive social relations).

Importantly, while most young people identify with particular peer groups, some of which are seen as distinct 'subcultural' formations (see Polk 1993; Denholm 1993), the sole identification with one particular group or style in a manner which is rigidly fixed over time is relatively unusual. Young people move around a lot—they mix with a wide variety of different peer groups (through sports, studies, neighbourhoods, family relations), and may engage in a wide variety of 'subcultural' activities in a relatively short period of time. Hebdige (1979, p. 122) captures the fluctuating nature of youth cultural and subcultural activity particularly well:

. . . different youths bring different degrees of commitment to a subculture. It can represent a major dimension in people's lives—an axis erected in the face of the family around which a secret and immaculate identity can be made to cohere—or it can be a slight distraction, a bit of light relief from the monotonous but none the less paramount realities of school, home and work. It can be used as a means of escape, of total detachment from the surrounding terrain, or as a way of fitting back in to it and settling down after a week-end or evening spent letting off steam.

To put it in slightly different terms, it is rare for most young people to actually adopt a visible, recognised subcultural lifestyle in the sense of an integrated deviant 'way of life'. Rather, most adopt the 'acceptable' cultural forms in a society. It is the fashions that revolve around a core centre of 'respectability' which change, not basic ways of living and relating to others.

The experience of social connection tends to transcend the shifting and activity-specific subcultural forms. That is, young people who connect positively with other members of their immediate family or community, or who have a particular relationship with home, school, church/religion, work and sport/leisure activity do so in ways which generally continue through (and regardless of) periods of conformity with or break from the dominant cultural conventions. Close social ties operate well beyond the dictates of fad or fashion, and are inclusive of those young people who do not continuously share in the broad aims of the mainstream social institutions.

While most young people tend to be fairly conventional in outlook and lifestyle, and to merely dabble in the subcultural realm, there are, nevertheless, distinct and enduring patterns of subcultural style and group formation. Here we can point to the specificity of distinct youth subcultural identities in certain places (including, bogans, punks, technos, skins, Rastas, psychobillies, hiphop). Some types of youth cultural practice thus do have a particular form and content which persist over time. Similarly, for some young people, there is a sense of permanency associated with subcultural identity, and a realisation that lifestyle is in fact inextricably intertwined with subcultural experience.

In such cases, the specific subcultures tend to be linked directly to social background (that is, according to the conjunction of class, ethnicity, gender). For example, African American is linked to hiphop, West Indian to Rasta, Anglo-Celtic to punk or skinhead; young males tend to have the higher public visibility across many of the 'spectacular' subcultural forms, although a number of groups (for example, gothics, psychobillies) appear to have more fluid rules about gender participation; there are class differences in the intensity and meaning of subcultural form (ranging from conventional to oppositional relationships to the status quo); and so on.

The adoption of particular subcultural styles is always a complex process involving a diverse range of influences. For example, on the one hand some street styles are not in fact unique to young people— they may provide important symbolic markers for a community as a whole, as with the practice of fixing hair into dreadlocks. Alternatively, some subcultural styles are promoted by the media and commercial interests as being specifically 'youth' styles. This may be done in order to sensationalise news or to build a market niche for certain products, for example wearing baseball caps on backwards. Either way, style becomes a type of superficial marker of difference between 'adult' and 'youth', one which dismisses the far greater continuity across generations in terms of gaining a livelihood.

CULTURAL FORMATION AND SOCIAL DIFFERENCE

Before discussing the substantive reasons for subcultural difference, it is useful to outline more fully the social processes which lie behind subcultural activity in general. Youth cultural activity, including subcultural activity, is a constant, dynamic process. It often revolves around an ongoing contestation over meaning and power involving the different sources of cultural ideas and identity available to a young person (such as the family, media, church, school, peers). Importantly, the process is dynamic not only in the sense of different and rapidly changing influences in one's cultural universe, but as well, with respect to the levels of participation by young people in actively constructing their cultural life.

In the first instance, how one sees oneself, how we dress, speak, act and relate to the wider social community is contingent upon the range of material resources open to us. For example, young people in remote farming communities have very different natural and social environments within which to interact than do urban young people. This will affect the immediate resources available to each group (for example, up-market shops for the latest fashion clothes, proximity to animals in their native habitat) and potential 'things to do' (attend pubs, clubs, schools, sports, or hang out in streets). Meanwhile, the world of the microchip has apparently eroded many other of the cultural barriers between city and country. Thus, the latest music, videos and movies from Hollywood are now in reach of anyone—in the whole world—who has the requisite transmission receiver equipment, regardless of geographical location or isolation.

A good illustration of this latter point is made by Brady (1992, pp. 1–2). Writing of young Aboriginal people in remote Australian communities, she says:

> Based on my own research observations it is possible to state that many young Aboriginal people in some of the most 'tradition oriented' of the bush townships now sport the trappings and display the 'style' of youth elsewhere: their clothing is determinedly different from that worn by adults; their hairstyles and jewellery, the music they listen to and their comportment—all these are in deliberate contradistinction to others around them. Television by satellite, local radio and TV stations, videos, cassette recorders, local rock bands and discos, are all features of everyday life in the deserts of Central Australia and the mangroves of the north.

Brady's observations about the impact of popular conceptions of youth on young Aboriginal people raises questions about the significance of cultural change in its broadest sense.

On the other hand, while the transmission of ideas has both speeded up in pace and collapsed the physical (and cultural) distances between people in different regions of the world due to technological development, the fact remains that what young people actually do with 'culture' is a contingent process. The focus on the relationship of young people to popular culture has tended to underplay the historically specific nature of this relationship, and its variations associated with social divisions such as gender, ethnicity and class.

Table 4.1   Processes of cultural formation and youth identity

Identity Through Consumption	Identity Through Production
Consumption of culture	Production of culture
Appropriation of culture	Reproduction of culture

In this sense, the cultural studies approach has taken for granted the idea that young people have a 'pre-social' self which they strive to develop and express through their engagement with mass media (Johnson 1993).

It is true that young people are influenced by myriad technologies, communities and histories. Yet, out of the many possible cultural options, it is the young people themselves who ultimately are implicated in determining what and how they want to be as 'cultural beings'. The construction of youth identity is thus not something which is simply done *to* young people—it involves a range of resources, choices and pressures.

Cultural formation is an uneven process, one which is conditioned by a wide range of situational factors (such as media access, geographical location, local amenities), personal preferences and choices (such as wanting to do one thing more than something else, to dress this way rather than that) and structural contexts (such as type of family formation, income level, institutional opportunities).

As a process, the construction of social identity involves a series of overlapping aspects (see table 5.1): the differential consumption of culture; the differential appropriation of culture; the differential production of culture; and the reproduction of cultural activity. The process of cultural formation means that identity is created, modified and reinforced through a series of consumption-related and production-related activities (see for examples, Hebdige 1979; Brake 1985; Corrigan 1979; Gilbert & Taylor 1991; McRobbie 1991; Johnson 1993).

Identity through consumption

Personal identity formation is a social phenomenon. It has a relatively passive dimension in that key cultural elements already exist (for example, family or community rituals and stories) or are produced for mass consumption (for example, television, advertising, pop music) in ways which preclude the young person themselves actually *doing* and *creating* new cultural forms. How we consume, however, is an integral part of the kind of person we are, and the kind of person we present to the wider world. Indeed, today youth itself is a consumable item, in that the superficial trappings of youth are now part of the consumer market (seen in, for example, the youthful aspect and appearance of Tina Turner or the selling of products designed for older people to 'feel and look young again').

Consumption of culture
In its restricted sense, the consumption of culture simply refers to a relatively passive response to cultural offerings such as media images, clothing fashions, music, and family and communal traditions and rituals which impact upon one's sexual, gender, ethnic and class sense of being. Mass produced 'culture' may be produced for some young people, but not all (for example, commercial definitions of audience needs and wants may target those with money). In the end, however, there are usually marked *social differences* in the consumption of music, videos, dance, and other cultural items in that different groups like different things. This denotes that there is an *active selection process* whereby different groups of young people tend to select different types of 'cultural elements' over others (for example, the type of music one listens to is associated with particular kinds of audiences). In this instance, then, identity is formed through relationship to particular kinds of friends, music, family ties, choice of movies, school subjects, and so on.

Appropriation of culture
We use the concept appropriation of culture to refer to a higher level of active and/or conscious use of cultural elements as part of the consumption process. For example, it is often the case that the 'buyer' has some autonomy in commercial transactions (how we consume is to some extent in our own hands). In other words, how we use what is offered for consumption is subject to manipulation, extension and *creative interpretation* by people (for example, performing new dances in the clubs, making 'waves' at the cricket match, older people buying 'youth'). What is 'consumed' thus takes on its own specific character depending upon who the consumer is. It hinges upon how young people incorporate what is on offer into their own cultural experiences (for example, media images of 'femininity' as expressed in middle class or working class role models evident in television programs such as 'Neighbours' or 'Melrose Place'). Identity is thus formed through the *active use of cultural symbols* which best reflect personal (family, friends) experience and which denote a shared connection with similarly placed people.

Identity through production

Consumption is a dynamic process. So, too, the production of culture by young people themselves is an active and dynamic process. Here, young people are directly implicated in the creation of new forms of cultural production. As such, how we produce and reproduce culture has a significant impact upon self-identity and group associations.

Production of culture

'The production of culture' refers to an active and *conscious relationship* to culture. This takes a number of different forms. For example, 'conventional' production might simply mean the use of existing cultural elements (of dress, of dance, of speaking, of relating to institutions) to forge novel trends that, while different, nevertheless remain within the boundaries of acceptable action (for example, tertiary students wearing gowns to class or inventing a new-look dress code as part of a fashion fad). Alternatively, 'counter-cultural' production constitutes a response to existing cultural life which rejects certain elements, and which celebrates difference for its own sake (as did the hippies of the 1960s). An 'oppositional cultural' production is that which not only rejects, but actively seeks to oppose and replace the existing cultural framework (as with the rule-breaking behaviour of punks, anarchists, skinheads, etc.). Identity is thus formed via the production of certain ways of being which establish the cultural location and visibility of the person *in relation to* other forms of cultural production.

Reproduction of culture

The reproduction of culture refers to activity which does not always imply or involve a conscious relationship to cultural formation. There are intended and *unintended consequences* of cultural production over time. As a process, we might find in some communities that there are ongoing 'magical' subcultural solutions to material problems based upon style (for example, spectacular subcultures such as Rastas or skinheads establish a visible identity for people on the margins of society). Similarly, and perhaps simultaneously, very often subcultures of rebellion (especially those centred on 'style') are incorporated into the dominant ideological framework through commercialisation (thus, the rebellious image is fine, as long as it signifies a musical rather than political trend). Nonetheless, there may exist emancipatory subcultures which are based upon conscious ideological and material challenges to the dominant cultural framework, centring on immediate identifiable political goals (for example, radical feminist or socialist youth). Identity formation is reproduced individually, at group level and at mass societal level in ways which reflect *different relationships to the dominant cultural framework*.

χ χ χ

How young people create, take on and change their identity(ies) is thus a complex process. It is a process featuring a high degree of social interaction, many diverse personal and institutional influences, and differing levels of consciousness and reflection.

The social construction of group difference is 'achieved' through a combination of the varied consumption, appropriation, production and reproduction of cultural elements. How cultural formation occurs in practice is in turn contingent upon one's social background—whether one is male or female, one's sexuality and sexual history, class background, ethnicity, nationality and 'race'—and in particular the ways in which families and communities teach people to enter into the processes of cultural formation (through traditions, stories, anecdotes, rituals, habits, forms of discipline, religious beliefs, political ideologies).

In assessing 'difference' we also have to be aware of the real and potential impact of the internationalisation (for example, via telecommunications) of particular cultural forms. As an instance, are we seeing the beginning of a new homogenous 'youth culture', primarily drawing upon US models and examples, which is traversing the globe via the information highway in all of its manifestations? If we take the above model of cultural formation (see table 5.1) as our starting point, then the answer would appear to be 'no'. At best, one might argue the case for a qualified 'yes'—but only insofar as any cultural process is dynamic, and will necessarily incorporate or react against the cultural elements prevalent in any time period.

CONFORMITY, ALIENATION AND RESISTANCE

The tendency in media treatments and youth studies research to both universalise and particularise youth experience in certain ways has important implications for the way in which the 'deviant' is defined. On the one hand, the trend towards universalising statements, especially on 'law and order' themes, reinforces the notion that all young people—young men especially—are potential offenders. A climate of suspicion, fear and trepidation is fostered in which young people generally are the main objects. In a similar vein, analysis which highlights the relative powerlessness of (all) young people, and which speaks of 'this generation' as being 'victims', serves to call forth images and responses that welfarise the problem and pathologise the young. In some cases, the 'offender' discourse and the 'victim' discourse explicitly cross over and overlap with each other—reinforcing the perception that young people themselves are indeed the problem and need to be dealt with via the strong arm (welfare and coercive divisions) of the state.

On the other hand, the situating of particularistic discourse (for example, of 'ethnic youth gangs') and case-study analysis (of specific subcultures) within the context of the universalist language (of 'youth as a problem') means that some young people will be targeted for state action even more than usual. And it is here that we see the conjunction of ideas relating to 'at risk' young people with perceptions of 'deviancy' relating to certain subcultural forms. This is evident in the manner in which media typifications (of 'gangs' or 'street kids', for example) and criminal justice responses to certain youth groups (indigenous young people or young people of colour, for example) exacerbate the stigmatisation of these young people. It opens the door to a broad range of technologies of surveillance and regulation designed to control specific sections of the youth population. These technologies and practices of social control are evident across different social domains, including the school, public venues, the street, shopping centres and increasingly the workplace.

Just as there are different degrees of attachment and participation in subcultural activity, so too there are different forms of powerlessness experienced by young people. The law(s) and education institutions, for example, position young people in society as dependent, less responsible and with fewer rights than older people. They may be 'socially constructed', but there are nevertheless real and lasting *age-based* divisions in society, which in many cases are experienced by young people across the social spectrum as unfair, unwarranted or simply unnecessary. Issues of conformity and opposition to these strictures are really matters of degree, rather than kind, when it comes to the general experiences of 'growing up' in societies with compulsory schooling. That is, it is not unusual to find most young people at some time complaining about or directly subverting age-related restrictions and expectations regarding their behaviour.

Beyond these feelings of relative powerlessness, however, there are of course deeper social divisions, more profound alienations and lack of power apparent within the wider population. Class differences and social divisions based upon gender and ethnicity still constitute the major defining and structuring influences in cultural and economic life. The objective positioning of young people in relation to these structural features ultimately determines the processes of their cultural formation (that is, how they respond to the elements identified in table 5.1), and their relationship to the dominant ideologies and institutions of society.

In more concrete terms, care has to be taken to differentiate the different types of and motivations for 'resistance' and 'opposition' exhibited by young people as influenced by social circumstance and age-based contradictions. For instance, we might point to those 'conformative' subcultures which celebrate 'difference' but which in reality do little to actually challenge the dominant ideas of capitalism, patriarchy and imperialism. Young people may be testing the boundaries of what is 'acceptable', but the contest is one which by and large simply demarcates 'youth' as a stage of dependence, as a time of transition to greater individual control and expression.

These conventional challenges to 'adult rule' can be distinguished from more radical 'subcultures of rebellion' which do overtly and directly attempt to critique the established order and its institutions (for example, rap music and 'cop bashing'). The experiential basis for such cultural forms stems from certain lived relationships (of racism, of poverty, of despair) which occasionally bubble up from the streets into the commercial cultural spheres. The involvement of youth in such subcultures is overlaid by the constant tension between a radicalised and a commercialised cultural expression.

This experience-derived subcultural expression is distinct yet again from a more politically motivated 'revolutionary subculture' which self-consciously adopts an ideology of emancipation (pertaining to politics of the left and the right). In the latter case, the form of 'cultural' expression is less important than the core political issues at stake. Nevertheless, it may be the case that the politicisation of young people occurs through involvement with a particular subcultural form (and vice versa in terms of youth politicising existing subcultural activities). As Moysey (1993, p. 11) puts it:

> Subcultures reflect a combination of alienation from society and a rebellion against society. The social views of these groups are mixed and eclectic. The same subculture can include ideas that range from revolutionary, to reactionary, to nihilist. At the same time some subcultures are identified with progressive or reactionary views. For example, skinheads are identified with racist views, punks with anarchist views, hippies with anti-war views, and so on.

The analytical task is to separate out the different types of 'rebellion' and organisation among young people, and to distinguish the basis for different types of youth cultural and subcultural activity.

However, conformity and resistance constitute not just a process which manifests itself in the form of distinct subcultures and subcultural activities. The relationship that young people have to certain institutions is not dependent upon subculture per se. Indeed, as pointed out earlier, the majority of young people are not 'full-time' subcultural figures with a strong identification with one particular form.

As various school-based studies over time have demonstrated (see Walker 1987; Willis 1977; Corrigan 1979; Gilbert & Taylor 1991; Blackman 1995), the relationship between certain groups of young people and social institutions such as schools is shaped by various cultural dimensions (in terms of the influence of class, gender and ethnic background in the construction of identity and behaviour). But adoption of a distinctive subcultural response is not necessarily a prevalent part of this cultural process. Ultimately how particular categories of young people relate to authority figures such as teachers and police depends upon their membership of wider communities (such as women, working class, African American).

It has to be recognised, as well, that in many cases the 'resistance' exerted by 'disadvantaged' young people is not necessarily *against* mainstream institutions but constitutes struggles for a place *within* them. Working class girls have attacked their teachers (and thereby been accused of being school resisters), for example, precisely because they value education and thus seek more attention from teachers (Walker 1993). Similarly, some street 'gangs' are adamant that what they really want is recognition of their graffiti as bona fide art (Forrester 1993).

CONCLUSION

In the end, it is almost a truism that most young people want to be taken seriously, and generally most want to be part of the mainstream of conventional society (defined broadly). However, the sense of powerlessness and alienation is socially differentiated, and is felt differently by young people as they engage in particular institutional processes. The degree of connection and disconnection from the mainstream social institutions is a crucial factor in the cultural life of young people, and their relationship to the dominant ideologies and values of society.

Cultural studies can tell us how young people relate to their world, and in particular how youth identity (or subjectivity) is formed in the crucible of family relations and institutional experience. Subcultural analysis can explain the ways in which young people attempt to 'resolve' the contradictions of their age and situation through distinctive activities and behaviour. Such studies only have purchase, however, if they in turn can point to some way in which young people generally (for example, via 'youth rights' strategies), and the marginalised in particular (for example, via issue-specific campaigns such as anti-racist strategies), can gain greater control over their lives.

In a world where the 'average person' is in fact losing control, and in many ways is being rendered less powerful than ever as an individual, it is clear that for the young person, as with the older, cultural activity needs to be linked to *collective identity* and *political action.* The terrain upon which such an identity and action can be constructed is that of the main 'institutions of transition'. It is here that the material circumstances and life opportunities of young people are mapped out into the future. It is also here that the potential for subversive, oppositional and liberating politics can be further developed. For how young people experience the social institutions can have a dramatic impact on their social, economic and political life. It is to consideration of these experiences that we now turn.

5 Youth transitions

The concept of *transition* has become central in discussions of youth, especially in the English speaking world, but increasingly also in European countries such as Germany, Norway and the Netherlands. The interest in understanding and in structuring transitions for young people has emerged in response to the failure of traditional pathways towards achieving adulthood. In Australia, Britain and in Canada the interest in youth transitions has focused on the relationship of education and schooling to the labour market.

The study of transitions focuses on the way in which institutions structure the process of growing up. Regardless of the nature of the formal and systematic processes, all societies are experiencing increasing divisions between those for whom a legitimate livelihood is achievable and those who become marginalised. Drawing on recent research our discussion focuses on three key areas: the failure of the education–work nexus in industrialised countries, the struggle to achieve a livelihood, and the development of the capacities for social practices which will enable full participation in society.

In the following sections we explore the uses and meanings of 'transition' as a descriptive concept and its use as a metaphor. We argue that in the advanced industrialised countries, it is evident that there are now wide gaps between the experiences of young people, especially some groups, and the policies that inform the institutional structuring of pathways and transitions to adulthood.

THE CONCEPT OF TRANSITION

The concept of 'youth transition' involves a duality—it has two dimensions which exist in a kind of tension. In a seeming contradiction, the concept of transition, which has the imagery of process, fluidity and change, has been harnessed to a static, categorical notion of youth. Hence, although we appear to be dealing with a concept which has change and process at its centre, it offers instead a perspective on youth as a steady progression through identifiable and predictable stages, to a set end point: adulthood. The transition stages are assumed to be commonly experienced by a majority of young people—a mainstream. For example, the transition from school to work, one of the central dimensions of transition to adulthood, is seen as the process whereby an individual is successful in gaining the credentials education has to offer and in negotiating the competitive labour market which structures opportunities.

There is, however, ample evidence that there is usually no definite point of arrival, that there are multiple processes of transition, and that they differ according to social division. Describing the experiences of young people in Britain, Chisholm comments that under some circumstances, which include educational failure, institutionalised discrimination and high unemployment, young people 'experience delayed, broken, highly fragmented and blocked transitions' (1993, p. 30). Looker's (1993) research on young rural women in Canada reveals that social context has a fundamental impact on the nature and meaning of the transition from school to work. For young women in rural areas, there are social costs associated with their decision to get a job, because it means moving away from their local area and away from important social connections. Other research (for example, Evans & Heinz 1993) offers comparisons of the ways in which different national education and training systems structure the process of transition for young people in different ways. As Chisholm (1993) points out, understanding the impact of institutionalised transition processes requires that cultural perspectives on the relationship between education, work and adult practices are taken into account. She argues that compared with Germany, there is a cultural tradition in Britain for young people to make an earlier transition into adulthood through getting a job.

What this research reveals is that there are multiple dimensions to the process of 'becoming adult'. The processes are not as systematic as they might seem, and the meaning of the different dimensions is very different depending on where young people are located, socially and geographically. Getting a job and moving away from home and from their community, for rural youth, is likely to put them in a far more ambiguous status than young people who are able to find employment in their local area. The focus on *independence* assumed to be associated with growing up sometimes obscures the extent to which interdependence is important to young people. Young people who do not have to move away from the city where their family and friends live to become employed have the option to negotiate the 'distance' between themselves and their families, including the frequency of social contact, and the extent to which they can rely on family and friends in an emergency.

The term 'transition to adulthood' draws on the idea that young people make one transition to adulthood, and that adulthood is a clearly defined status—a destination at which one 'arrives'. Even the versions of transition which allow more complexity by referring to the plural 'transitions to adulthood' remain fixed on the notion that there are definite markers. For example, these 'transitions' are often signalled by events such as leaving school, leaving home, getting married, having children or getting a job. Other markers of arrival at significant points may include reaching menarche or one's first sexual experience. While each of these events does mark a point of transition from one state or condition into another, the complexity in using them categorically is that their meaning is not necessarily consistent across all groups, they do not necessarily mark a significant change, and finally, they do not remain fixed.

One of the central issues in understanding youth transitions is that many of the above 'markers' of adult life are transitory, reversible and impermanent. Leaving home is a notoriously tenuous process for many young people. Research on this aspect of the transition to adulthood has found that a significant phenomenon is 'boomerang children', who leave home only to return time and time again. Getting married also has an increasingly uncertain status, because 'de facto' coupling arrangements are legally and socially as significant as marriage and because both arrangements have a relatively high rate of breakdown (now one in three marriages in Australia result in divorce). Leaving school (and returning) is also increasingly an ongoing process, as life-long education has become a more common experience. Even the transition to parenthood is an uncertain status, evidenced by the ease with which substantial numbers of parents avoid both their children and their financial and social obligations to them.

Of all of the signifiers of adulthood, getting a job is fundamental and yet this aspect is also most notoriously ambiguous. Many children are already engaged in paid work outside the home. In some countries, for example in Brazil in the rural areas surrounding San Paulo, children may be as young as eight or nine when they are employed in local factories. In Australia, Canada and Britain, it is now common for school children to be employed. For example, in

Australia, around one-third of secondary school children aged 17 years are employed. At the same time, industrial and workplace restructuring, recession and the impact of global labour markets have meant that many adults do not have employment. If we use these points of transition as the markers of achieving adult status, does their loss also mean loss of adult status? Does the arrival at a particular marker mean the same thing for young people in different countries and within different social locations? For example, completing secondary school has a different meaning for youth in Germany than it does for youth in Australia or in Britain. In each of these countries, completing secondary education also has very different meanings for young women, compared with their male counterparts. When we examine the realities of the 'transitions to adulthood' (see table 6.1) it is clear that the process itself is full of complexities which undermine notions of both youth and adulthood as discrete categories.

The use of a concept of transitions which assumes that the process is simply from 'youth' to 'adulthood' does not take sufficient account of these complexities—of the multiple transitions involved, their synchrony, and the circularity (or more accurately, the spiralling nature) of the processes of 'arrival' and 'departure' at different statuses throughout life—leaving and re-entering education or moving from employment to unemployment.

Furthermore, the concept of transitions is most closely related to a horizontal perspective of social life, in which youth as a life stage is emphasised at the expense of seeing that the experiences, interests and perspectives of young people are integrally related to those of other people who share their social location. The inclusion of a vertical frame of reference would take account of generational continuities, between women, men, and in terms of geographical location and cultural identification. Chisholm (1990) visualises a Rubic cube to illustrate a framework which includes age as well as intergenerational connections. Although young people do have some things in common because of their age, social divisions as well as geographical location locate young people in close connection with older people who share these social circumstances. The age connection between young people is the horizontal plane, and the social division, intergenerational connection between young people and others is the vertical plane. The following table illustrates this point.

The inclusion of the vertical plane adds an important dimension. Firstly, it draws attention to the presence of social divisions in young people's lives, and by implication, as something with which they struggle in the present, not just in the future. Secondly, it provides a frame of reference within which continuity can be conceptualised. In a survey of research on transitions beyond youth, De Vaus (1995)

Table 5.1   Dimensions of youth transitions

Horizontal (age)	Vertical (generation/culture)
Common experiences based on age, e.g., popular music or style, which are expressed in youth subcultures	Commonalities with older people in one's community; young people gain knowledge about their cultures, e.g., Aboriginal cultures or migrant cultures
Compulsory education	Social and cultural understandings about education and school knowledge inherited through family experience
Entering history at a particular time, (e.g., experiencing the Vietnam war, being present at the destruction of the Berlin Wall, witnessing the last testing of nuclear warheads in the Pacific	Specific positioning within historical processes through culture and family, e.g., refugees from the Balkans war
Decimated youth labour market	Family and neighbourhood networks linking young people with employment

comments that it has been a common assumption that people will predictably pass through a standard set of stages in a fairly uniform way throughout their lives. His review reveals that the evidence for life-cycle stages which are predictable and uniform is rather thin and can only be sustained by ignoring the complexity of human interaction. Instead, De Vaus points out that, 'relationships are marked far more by continuity than by change, and as far as can be gleaned from people's accounts of growing up, the basic character of relationships in adulthood is much the same as in childhood and adolescence' (1995, p. 29).

Yet, despite its limitations, the concept of transition is used because it offers a metaphor for the process of growing up. The following section explores this use of the concept.

THE METAPHOR OF TRANSITION

To say that transition offers a metaphor for describing the process of growing up is to expose the assumptions underlying its use. Table 6.2 identifies some of the key aspects of the metaphor of youth transition, and compares them with the patterns which are emerging from the research on young people's experiences.

The metaphor of pathways is very clearly apparent in the education and training discourses in Australia (Finn 1991). 'Pathways'

Table 5.2   Transition as metaphor

Metaphor of transition	Experience of growing up
Linear process, e.g., school to work	Cyclical process, e.g., school to work to school to work
Uni-dimensional, e.g., establishing work skills	Multidimensional, e.g., establishing livelihood, sexuality, identity
Points of arrival, e.g., first job	Always becoming, e.g., changing jobs, changing relationships
Circumscribed by biological age	Social meaning of age
Horizontal dimension, with emphasis on contemporaries	Vertical and horizontal dimensions, whereby age intersects with generation

adds to the metaphor of transitions, a kind of 'outdoor' component, conveying an image of different 'roads' to be chosen in leaving one sheltered position (compulsory schooling) and in arriving and becoming established in another (a job).

This metaphorical use of the idea of transitions positions young people as individual viewers of the landscape on which the pathways are visible and accessible. Young people make their individual choices (after reading the relevant 'maps' or talking to travellers who have gone there before) and take their 'paths' towards their destinations. The paths are assumed to be there, so if some young people do not make it to the destination, the fault lies with them. In this way, the metaphor of transitions effectively individualises the process of growing up, and its outcomes. The 'pathways' (institutionalised processes, such as particular courses of education or training) are well trodden by the 'mainstream' of young people. Those who do not fit into the processes are described as 'at risk'.

A further aspect of the metaphorical view of transitions as pathways which young people take, is that it is assumed that the outcomes are necessarily predictable and equitable. It is seldom recognised that the first experiences that many young people have in the labour market and in attempting to live independently may be those of exploitation.

An alternative language, which nonetheless draws on a similar metaphorical base to describe the processes of growing up is that of 'status passage' and 'life course'. These concepts have been especially prominent in the German literature and research on young people (Heinz 1991). The advantage of using the idea of 'life course' is that it offers a perspective that does not assume that adulthood is an arrival point, but instead that there is a continuum throughout life, involving changes in status. However, in practice, this concept also tends to draw on a linear notion of life stages.

In the German literature, the notion of a life course is closely aligned to the notion that individuals are 'at risk' of not conforming to institutionalised processes. The potential exists within the 'life course' framework to understand the multiple dimensions of the transition towards adult life. However, it tends to be used largely as a descriptive tool, which ignores the power relations which operate when groups of young people are systematically marginalised by institutions. Although each society does offer a range of options to young people, the extent to which young people's eventual experiences of growing up can be seen in terms of a coherent and systematic series of pathways and linking transitions would seem to be very limited.

In the research literature on youth transitions it is clear that the concept of transition is most useful in conveying the 'big picture'. It offers a framework for describing the patterns created by the institutionalised processing of young people. There are several ways in which these patterns can be interpreted. One is to turn the focus to young people, describing the characteristics and experiences of those who fail, become marginal or are 'at risk', compared with those who are successful. Focusing on the young people who are not successful ends up locating the reasons for their failure in their own characteristics. So, for example, young women are assumed to have a 'domestic orientation' or working class young men themselves fail to gain the credentials needed to enter the apprenticeships they want. While these observations may be accurate, they fail to grasp how institutions (for example, schools and training programs) systematically create and reinforce these unequal outcomes through their classed and gendered practices.

Another approach is to explore the social and economic processes and practices that marginalise young people through the stages of transition. This approach, by contrast, recognises that the source of transition blockages, ruptures and dead ends are not in the characteristics of young people, but in the restructuring and restructured economies and the institutions that structure the transition processes.

Both approaches are clearly important in understanding the contemporary experience of growing up. However, the tendency to focus on young people 'in transition', on their risks and individual choices—predominant in youth studies—offers only a partial understanding, and itself brings the risk of blaming those who have become marginalised.

TRANSITION AND EDUCATION

In all industrialised countries, education and training is now the central formal mechanism for structuring transition processes for young people. Given the importance of education in young people's lives, it is useful to explore these processes in more detail. Our interest is twofold. We aim to provide an overview of the different mechanisms for structuring transitions, and at the same time to come to an understanding of the experiences of different groups of young people which reflect social divisions. In this section we look at the differential impact of formal education and training systems, and in particular, its role in systematically marginalising some groups of young people.

Our discussion is informed by the recent literature on youth transitions which explores these issues in local contexts (for example, studies of Canadian youth in transition) and that which attempts to take a comparative approach (for example, studies of youth transitions in European countries). One of the issues with which we have had to contend is that the studies themselves emerge from distinctive research and theoretical traditions which need to be taken into account. Similarly, in her comparison of youth research in Britain and West Germany, Chisholm notes that there are distinctive 'cross-national' differences in the study of childhood and youth (Chisholm 1990, p. 11).

Studies of transitions in Britain have been informed by longitudinal studies which map the experiences young people have in the labour market and in education after they leave school. A tradition of longitudinal research based on large-scale surveys of young people's labour market and training patterns has emerged (for example, Evans & Heinz 1993) to complement the earlier ethnographic studies of transitions (see Finn 1987).

One of the consequences of the move towards larger scale surveys in Britain has been the increased potential to compare the experiences and trajectories of young people in that country with those in other countries for which there exist comparative large-scale data. Although these quantitative descriptive studies necessarily overlook much of the complexity and detail that is provided in smaller scale studies of young people's experiences, they do give an idea of broad patterns and of the connections between institutional processes and outcomes for young people.

Increasingly, large-scale research is being combined with qualitative research, offering an approach of greater analytical and explanatory potential. Comparing the transitions to the labour market for groups of young people in two regions in Germany and two in Britain, Evans and Heinz (1993) offer some interesting insights into transition processes and experiences. Young people in a region with an expanding labour market and others in a contracting labour market (in 1989) in Britain were matched and compared with their counterparts in Germany. Adding even more complexity, the study took account of the different segments within these labour markets, such as professional, skilled and semi-skilled occupations, comparing the routes taken by young people who entered different segments in each country. Evans and Heinz identified categories of school-to-work transition categories (career trajectories) which were broadly comparable in the two countries. These were:

1 Academic mainstream, leading towards higher education, training and education, and professional occupations.
2 Training and education leading to skilled employment: dual system in Germany; work-based training, apprenticeships or further education leading to vocational qualifications in England.
3 Other forms of education and training leading particularly to semi-skilled employment.
4 Early labour market experience of unskilled jobs, unemployment and short-term remedial training schemes (Evans & Heinz 1993, p. 148).

Different forms of education, training and experience were mapped onto these broad trajectories, but most importantly, the young people were asked questions about the quality of their education or training for work. They were asked if they had gained useful skills, carried responsibility and been challenged by their experiences of education, training and work, after the compulsory years (post-16 years of age). A brief outline of the main features of each 'system' of education and training will provide a useful backdrop for the findings reported by Evans and Heinz.

One of the central features of the German education and training system (developed in West Germany) is its *high level of institutionalisation*. For young people, this system has offered a tradition in which there is a high level of certainty in the process (and until relatively recently, in the outcomes) of education and training. From the point of view of many in English speaking countries, in which the processes of transition to work have traditionally been far more individualised, the German system has been seen to offer many advantages. In fact, as Green comments (1991, p. 328), 'there has long been the suspicion that some aspects are better managed on the continent'. In this context, the surprising aspect of the results by Evans and Heinz are that the German youth in their study were not necessarily advantaged by their education and training, compared with the young people in Britain.

The system established in West Germany in 1969 builds on a three-pronged schooling system, consisting of the *Realschule*, the *Hauptschule* and the *Gymnasium*. Students leaving the *Realschule* at 16 or 17, and those leaving the *Hauptschule* at 15 or 16 (and less frequently, those graduating from the *Gymnasium*) enter a formal system of vocational training. The system is entered by gaining employment with an employer who is licensed to provide training. As described by Green (1991), these young people will then spend up to three and a half years in on-the-job training, which involves one or two days a week at the *Berufsschule*, a vocational college, where they continue both with a general education and receive vocational education. This system has traditionally served around 65 per cent of young people, of whom an overwhelming majority (around 90 per cent) receive a vocational qualification, after undergoing practical and written assessments.

From the point of view of other countries, one of the most interesting features of this system is that it depends on the collaboration of employers, who invest in it, as well as the government, employer organisations, unions and educationalists. The system also has a number of weaknesses. Two which are regularly identified are the rigid nature of the dual system of education and training, and the seeming impermeability of gender divisions in this form of training. The system of vocational training has not served in the best interests of many women, locating women in the traditional trades of hairdressing, retail and clerical work, and in the lower status and less well paid traineeships (Green 1991).

Britain, unlike Germany, has no formal, institutionalised process linking levels and kinds of education and training with labour markets or occupational sectors. Formal qualifications tend only to give access to the professional end of the occupational ladder. Young people leave school on average two years earlier than their German counterparts, and generally *negotiate the labour market as an individual process*. Some young people obtain apprenticeships (mainly young men), but a majority who leave school directly after completing the compulsory years enter a secondary labour market of low-skill, short-term and often dead-end jobs. These jobs are very different from those in the primary labour market, which involve high skill, often extensive training and favourable employment conditions. In the British system:

> the links between the educational system and the labour market are
> dominated by the small apprenticeship system, which provides a
> highly structured status passage for the minority who are successful
> in the competition for entry to it (Ashton & Sung 1991, p. 40).

The tradition of comparatively early school-leaving in Britain, combined with the restructuring of labour markets, and in some areas the almost total collapse of youth labour markets, has meant that young people in some locations are highly vulnerable. In the context of a tradition that does not hold school in high regard, their 'pathways' to establishing a legitimate livelihood are jeopardised.

Partly in response to the plight of young people in regions of high unemployment, the Youth Training Scheme was introduced in Britain in the early 1980s. Although this scheme was introduced amid rhetoric about creating bridges to employment, in reality the scheme has tended to be only tenuously linked with sustaining work (Finn 1987).

The unexpected results of the Evans and Heinz research comparing the job outcomes for school leavers in Germany and in Britain were that the young people in both the contracting and expanding labour markets in Britain were more likely to feel that they had gained useful skills from their education, had carried responsibility and had been challenged by their education than their German counterparts. There were also differences in the value orientations to work, education and career. The German respondents were reported to feel more sceptical about job prospects, and to have a sense of being somewhat marginal. By contrast, the English respondents had 'more flexible job orientations combined with optimism about their future prospects even in the contracting labour markets' (Evans & Heinz 1993, p. 152).

Young people in Britain, then, were forced to engage with the labour market on an individual basis much earlier than the young people in Germany with whom they were compared, and their attitudes reflected this. The actual trajectories of the young people in Britain that were documented in this study show that some very unpredictable 'careers' were negotiated. For example, 'a young woman left school with two General Certificate of Education (GCE) subjects at advanced level to work in an insurance office, but became dissatisfied with her prospects, took a second chance and went off to train as a teacher' (Evans & Heinz 1993, p. 156). Evans and Heinz comment that these outcomes were very unlikely to have occurred in the German system.

However, while the 'flexibility' of the lack of institutional arrangements in Britain does allow some individuals to negotiate positive outcomes for themselves, this does not address the issue of how young people will establish a livelihood in locations and regions where the labour market offers few options. Furthermore, because of the highly segmented nature of the labour market in Britain (Ashton & Sung 1991), young people negotiating their future place in the workforce are highly disadvantaged once they enter the secondary labour market. In fact, it would be inaccurate to call the British arrangement a 'system' in the same way that the German institutionalised process operates. Like in Australia, there is little systematic linking of education, training and employment except at the professional levels, and even though young people may have a positive outlook, be good negotiators and able to take responsibilities, the lack of a coherent framework is indeed confusing for some, and ultimately the result is that they are marginalised.

The evidence of the outcomes of the institutionalised transition framework of the German system is that it offers some groups of young people an extended time (and space) in which they gradually move into employment. Schooling is an accepted part of early adult life in Germany and it is expected that young people will take until into their twenties to find a job. There is evidence that young people who have taken the apprenticeship 'pathway' through education have a relatively high employment rate, even in local areas which have a high unemployment rate. Longitudinal research on the experiences of a sample of apprentices in the German region of Bremen found that although only 46 per cent of skilled workers were still working in the occupation for which they had been trained after five years, overall unemployment in this group was quite low (at 4 per cent), and 83 per cent had been offered employment *in their training firm* after the apprenticeship (Monnich & Witzel 1995). However, there is also evidence that this system has a rigid structure, in which social divisions, especially those based on gender are perpetuated (Green 1991). The system of occupational training, in particular, works in a highly gendered way to the disadvantage of young women.

The comparison of the experiences of some groups of young people in Britain with those in Germany provides an insight into how institutionalised processes (and the lack thereof) directly affect young people's experiences and approaches to leaving school and to getting a job. It is clear from this study that institutional processes as well as cultural traditions have a role. This is especially evident in the preference many young people in the British study had for leaving school almost directly after the compulsory years were dispensed with, and entering the labour market, even in circumstances where the labour market was not buoyant.

Recent Canadian research suggests that young people in Canada have responded to changes in the youth labour market by staying on at school and by making a series of transitions from school to the labour market and back to school for a period (Krahn 1991). Krahn reports that in the late 1980s, 77 per cent of high school graduates in a study of young people in three Canadian cities continued their education. Compared with young people in Britain the Canadian youth were less likely to go into a training scheme and more likely to prolong their education, combining further education with part-time work. This study found that although part-time work was available, the quality of the work was poor, especially for young people entering the secondary part of the segmented labour market. Gender-based occupational segmentation continues to be a feature of the transition process for young people in Canada too (Mandell & Crysdale 1993). Young women are more likely to enter a narrow range of occupations, and to be limited to the lower echelons of the occupations they enter.

For young people in Canada, establishing a livelihood has become a rather drawn out process. A majority prolong their education well beyond secondary school as educational credentials increasingly offer a point of entry into the primary labour market of professional, well-paid and relatively secure jobs.

In each of the countries which have been briefly surveyed here, it is clear that although the transitions into employment from school are different, they could all be described as an extended, uncertain and at times fragmented process of transition. However, what is missing from the broad sweep necessary to understand how formal processes (or the lack of them) structure the parameters of the transition process is a more detailed picture of what happens to young people who are the casualties of institutionalised processes that systematically marginalises some groups at the same time as supporting others. We need to grasp the ways in which institutions contribute to the production of inequalities. The following section addresses this issue by discussing the issue of early school-leaving for young Australians.

TRANSITION AND LIVELIHOOD

The experiences of early school-leavers reveal how the formal transition process of education actively marginalises young people from low socioeconomic backgrounds. In Australia, this pattern endures, despite a concerted effort on the part of the government to increase the number of young people remaining at secondary school or in some form of training until they are 18 years old. In the Australian research on early school-leavers, we begin to get an insight into the maintenance and perpetuation of social divisions based on class and gender.

The substantial overall growth in the numbers of young people completing secondary school in Australia has meant that the final-year student population has broadened. Participation in year 12 has become a mass rather than a minority experience. Groups of young people previously unrepresented in post-compulsory schooling (such as young women, and young people from working class backgrounds) are now represented in greater proportions.

However, many of these young people who complete year 12 are refugees from the labour market. Their participation in post-compulsory education does not reflect a significant change in the value placed on education. More importantly, because of the deterioration of the youth labour market, increased levels of educational participation do not necessarily greatly improve outcomes. The process of *escalating credentialism* changes the meaning that educational credentials have in the labour market. Inevitably some school completers are only marginally advantaged in the competition for low-skill, short-term jobs and for places in further education with early school-leavers (Wyn & Lamb 1996).

Patterns of early school-leaving in Australia reveal that young people from working class backgrounds constitute the vast majority of those leaving school early. Although the absolute numbers of early school-leavers have declined over the last decade, they remain a distinctive group. Young people who leave school early are likely to be seriously disadvantaged in an increasingly competitive labour market (Department of Employment, Education & Training 1989). Early school-leavers are now more likely than ever to experience extended periods of unemployment, to take up short-term, unskilled work, to fail to obtain an immediate post-school qualification and to miss out in the competition for a base-level traineeship, and to remain dependent for long periods on government and other welfare assistance. In the current economic climate, this means that a significant proportion of young people are destined to live in poverty.

In a comprehensive analysis of data from the Australian Longitudinal Survey (ALS) and the Australian Youth Survey (AYS) the Youth Research Centre analysed the early school-leaver cohorts in the total samples to determine their profiles and ways in which their constitution had changed since 1985. The findings indicated that there has been little change in the social and class groupings of early school-leavers since the initial rise in school retention rates. Early school-leavers still come from the same types of family and schooling background that characterised educational inequality before the changes in policy.

The Youth Research Centre's analysis revealed that in 1988, a majority of young women who left school before completing year 12 (76.7 per cent) and young men (79.1 per cent) were from families where the father's occupation was skilled or unskilled manual work. Over three-quarters of the young men and young women came from families where the mother had no post-secondary education herself.

Amongst early school-leavers in 1988, young women and young men took up different options, along traditional gender lines, with a majority of young women going into sales and related work (52.9 per cent, compared with 9.2 per cent of the young men), and young men into apprenticeships (42.9 per cent) and labouring work (37.8 per cent).

The research on early school-leavers and their trajectories provides an insight into the contribution of educational processes to the alienation of this significant group of young people. Young people who leave school early are seriously disadvantaged for two reasons. Firstly, the labour market in which they seek jobs is the secondary labour market of part-time, short-term contract jobs, with little continuity and poor conditions (Whyte & Probert 1991; Wilson 1992; Sweet 1992). Secondly, pathways back into education and training are not easy for them to gain access to. Early school-leavers have been displaced within the Technical and Further Education (TAFE) by young people who complete their secondary schooling in that system. It also seems that many early school-leavers find it difficult to complete their secondary education, even if they do 're-enter' school (Holden 1992).

The situation for young women who leave school early is even worse than for their male counterparts. A longitudinal study of 132 early school-leavers from the state of Victoria revealed that there were few clear 'pathways' that these young people—both male and female—followed. Few maintained employment over the entire three years, and most drifted in and out of part-time or short-term jobs, and relied on income support or on family or friends (Holden 1992).

Within this general picture, the patterns for young women were different from those for young men. Only 17 per cent of the young women in the study were exclusively on an employment pathway in comparison with 30 per cent of the young men. While none of the young men was exclusively on an income-support pathway, 6 per cent of the young women had been mostly on either unemployment benefits or a sole-parent pension.

Of the remaining 77 per cent of the young women, it was difficult to discern any clear patterns in terms of pathways. What was evident was a marked tendency to chop and change amongst options and to gain little from attempts to return to school to take on further education. Movement between jobs also did not appear to reflect any consistent type of pathway. The link between jobs and further education was minimal.

Young women who were not in employment found it difficult to gain access to and remain in the labour market. By comparison, young men were able to move more easily between jobs and other options. They were able to spend varying amounts of time dependent on their families, receiving unemployment benefits or without a means of support before returning to the labour force or to education and training.

Overall, young women were more likely to be unemployed or employed in positions which did not provide an adequate living wage. The employed tended to be working in sectors of the labour market which did not offer job security or the chance for advancement or career development. Young women were also more likely to be living independently of their parents and unlikely to return to the family home when their financial situation weakened. Living away from home also increased their cost of living with the need to establish and maintain a place of residence.

Early school-leavings raises an important question about the formal transition processes in the Australian context: how can education and training be structured to ensure equality of outcomes for all young people (see Wyn & Wilson 1993)? In the current system, there are few institutionalised processes whereby these young people can regain a foothold on the difficult terrain of the labour market once they have left school early. Unlike the young British people described by Evans and Heinz (1993) who were apparently able to make a number of flexible and creative job and training moves once they had made an early entry into the labour market, Australian early school-leavers are in one sense 'locked out' of the formal economy (see figure 3.2). The structures of both post-compulsory education and training, and of the labour market, instead of creating openings or pathways which lead to security and independence, effectively foreclose their options.

POLICY RESPONSES

The experience of early school-leavers in Australia highlights one of the most fundamental issues about the processes of transition to adulthood. That is, during the last 20 years, the processes involved in 'growing up' and establishing a livelihood have undergone fundamental change. The traditional processes, such as finding a job, have become much more complicated, as the labour markets in all countries have been subjected to change. Although economic and labour market restructuring has had an impact on all groups, it has had a specific effect on young people, some of whom, as the Australian research illustrates, are systematically denied access to establishing a livelihood.

It is in this context that policy-makers have sought to ameliorate the situation for young people. Researchers, including many of those identified in the above discussion, have contributed to our understanding of the production of inequality by exploring the processes and outcomes of formal transition processes in order to identify what works, what doesn't work, for whom, and where the gaps are. This is not to imply that the issues we have raised here are simply amenable to a 'technical' solution, ignoring the politics of inequality. On the contrary, many researchers have placed education at the centre of the political process of 'transition' in advocating approaches to schooling that acknowledge poverty, class, gender and other social divisions (for example, Kenway et al. 1994; Yates 1993; Connell 1994).

Although our discussion has focused on Australian early school-leavers, similar processes affect young people in other countries. For example, Chisholm (1995) has identified the failure of formal transition processes across Europe as a 'system default'. Even those young people who have educational credentials are not guaranteed access to employment, and 'the only sure-fire bet is that the unqualified and the least qualified are falling ever further behind into long-term marginalisation and exclusion' (Chisholm 1995, p. 284). The challenge is to develop policies which are based on the different realities of young people's lives, rather than on a fictional mainstream.

In the Australian research on early school-leavers, there is a very clear message to policy-makers. A gap exists between the policy rhetoric of having a high level of participation in post-compulsory education, and the reality for the substantial group who continue to seek direct entry into the labour market. The major policy response has been one of 'retention', not so much through making schooling more palatable to those who would rather not be there, but through the economic necessity that until the age of 18, young people cannot obtain unemployment benefit, but they can obtain 'Austudy', a means-tested social security measure which enables young people to remain at school.

In Britain, education and training has also become the main policy response to the changing circumstances within which young people grow up. Young people in Britain continue to leave school relatively early (two years before their German counterparts), and to negotiate the labour market as individuals. However, as in the Australian situation, there is a sizeable group of young people who do not fare well in these circumstances. The research on the Youth Training Scheme, much of which was carried out in the 1980s, reveals that for many of these young people, the government policy of providing training simply resulted in the accumulation of credentials which appeared to have little value in establishing a foothold on the competitive and restricted labour market for young people (Finn 1987). Others have commented on the relative lack of education and training opportunities in England, compared with the United States, Japan and France (for example, Green 1991).

The extent of interest in 'transitions' in the Canadian research on young people indicates that there are problems there too. For a proportion of young Canadians, an extended period of education, punctuated by short-term jobs is an accepted 'pathway' to establishing a livelihood. However, like the Australian experience, the research indicates that in the present circumstances the education and training option as a policy response only serves a particular group. The Canadian research on young people in transition to adulthood reveals that young women (Looker 1993; Mandell & Crysdale 1993), blacks (James 1993) and young people from first nations communities (Webster & Nabigon 1993) are systematically marginalised through these processes.

Although the West German tradition of education and training offers a more extended and secure 'space' within which a majority of young German people are able to make their transition towards establishing a livelihood, there is a growing awareness that there are some groups who 'slip through' this system, who become marginal.

Policy responses to the changed circumstances of young people in all industrialised countries will have to take account of the new shape of inequality and the ways in which class and gender relations and 'race' and ethnicity shape the outcomes of young people in each country in different ways. In the European context, the tensions caused by increasingly closer economic ties and the simultaneous reinforcement of local identifications have strong implications for education and training policy. As Chisholm comments:

> Young people living in Amsterdam, Berlin, Helsinki, Paris, London and Lisbon already share much as far as their material circumstances and ways of life are concerned; not everything, to be sure, but placing them in proximity and comparison is a good deal more sensible than talking about (for example) 'British youth' as if it were a homogeneous group in relation to other national groups . . . The question that remains is whether, given these developments, the privileged position of *national* educational policy making will continue to make sense in the coming decade (1993, p. 8).

Chisholm concludes that the most important basis for educational policy is 'taking young people and their lives into serious account' (1993, p. 8). The challenge for policy is that once young people's lives are taken seriously, it is impossible to retain the comfortable notion that there exists a mainstream of young people who will be served by a policy oriented towards a homogeneous population. The emerging picture of the gaps in the institutionalised processes of transition into adult life in Australia reinforce the point Chisholm is making. We would like to briefly return to the early school-leavers, Australia's 'outsiders', to illustrate the implications of having education and training policies that respond to the reality of all young people's lives.

The reason for leaving school for the majority of early school-leavers in Australia is that they are dissatisfied with school. Early school-leaving is consistently associated with the 'push' of a negative experience of school rather than with the 'pull' of a good job or a clear concept of how to establish a legitimate livelihood. Among the main factors identified in the literature are dissatisfaction with school work and school organisation, and poor relationships with teachers (Batten & Girling–Butcher 1981; Office of Youth Affairs 1978; Batten & Russell 1995; Holden & Dwyer 1992). This finding is significant because it focuses attention on the nature of schooling itself.

The provision of a curriculum which acknowledges the needs of young people who at present leave school early remains one of the most important challenges to education and training policy in Australia. The current post-compulsory education system has simply been attached to an already established post-compulsory education system for an elite who were graduating to tertiary education alone. Such a system would have to undergo fundamental change if it were to provide a worthwhile educational setting for the diversity of cultural, technical and social needs of the full range of young people in Australia.

Direct entry to the labour market will remain an attractive option for many, simply for economic reasons, and will offer a viable pathway for some. However, for the reasons discussed above, this option is most likely to lead to serious disadvantage in the longer term. Both remaining within secondary education, and re-entering secondary education or training are options that need to be more flexible and more accessible for all young people. In addition, more diverse links need to be established amongst the different parts of the post-compulsory education sector.

Education and training policy itself is an area of intense debate in Australia (Dwyer 1995; Marginson 1993; Taylor & Henry 1994; Wyn & Lamb 1996). Much of the concern centres on the nature of the curriculum and the extent to which equity and participation are taken seriously. From the 1980s onwards, many of the initiatives to make the curriculum relevant to a wider group of young people were oriented towards making closer links between schooling and work (Warner 1992; Freeland 1992). Career and work experience programs became widespread (Anderson 1983). In the education and training policy of the 1990s, this curriculum orientation has become focused on the linking of certain practices and skills with 'competencies' which describe particular outcomes from education and are seen to fit with the demands of employers in the workplace (Carmichael 1992).

Ironically, the very changes to the curriculum which were initiated because of a concern that educational programs were alienating groups of young people, have been replaced by a limited educational agenda. Collins (1992) argues that the post-compulsory curriculum in Australia has become increasingly narrow, instrumental and anti-intellectual. Freeland (1992) takes up the specific issue of the narrowness of the curriculum, arguing that the relationship between education and work seen in a limited, instrumental way tends to ignore the social meaning of work for all people, both paid and unpaid.

Others, such as Poole (1992), Sweet (1983), Burke (1983) and White (1990) have questioned the value of a curriculum which emphasises the supposedly instrumental relationship education has to employment. Poole stresses instead the importance of a broad, general curriculum in which young people are empowered to question the meaning of work in their lives and to understand the social, historical and cultural processes which have shaped the development of society, so that they may become involved in the negotiation of their future. This view is especially relevant in the context of the significant changes in the nature and quality of work as a result of Australian industrial, workplace and wage award restructuring.

The transition towards adult life also involves the negotiation of 'personal' dimensions of life, such as health and human relationships, including sexuality and drug use (Wyn 1993; Graetz 1992). Relationships with those in the workplace, as well as with other adults and young people in the community and family life are also important. Participation is also a significant dimension of the transition to adulthood. It refers to formal political knowledge and interest, participation in decision-making in educational institutions and in trade unions, and involvement in community action (Dwyer et al. 1984; Poole 1992). In each of these areas, social and structural change presents challenges which are only marginally addressed in the formal curriculum suggested in the current education and training policies and which many young people are ill equipped to meet. As Batten (1989) argues, the challenges facing young people require a post-compulsory curriculum that reflects a breadth of studies; a focus on student cooperation rather than competition and on personal as well as academic development.

In the following section, we address these 'forgotten dimensions' of the transitions to adulthood. As the broader policy responses to the changed circumstances of young people have become gradually subsumed within educational and training policy, the full complexity of 'becoming adult' has become more and more reduced to the narrow confines of technical competencies and the educational discourses dominated by the concern to manage the institutional processes. Within this discourse, education and training policymakers envisage that all young people are being trained for a future on the 'Starship Enterprise', in which complete dedication to paid work is the only rationale for life, and the void regarding personal relationships, domestic labour and the link between reproductive and productive, and paid and unpaid, labour is greater than space itself.

SOCIAL PRACTICES

Although leaving school and getting a job is an important aspect of growing up, it needs to be seen in the context of many other dimensions of life. Even the decision to leave school or to get a job is contingent on a range of other factors and circumstances in young people's lives. For young people 'getting a life' is about personal relationships, belonging in their community, and making a contribution as well as having a good income. These priorities are not just held with regard to the future—they are relevant to the present of young people's lives. When asked about their thoughts on school, young people in Australia in a study by Wilson and Wyn consistently gave the response that school was about preparing to get a good job, and about friendship. The research by Wilson and Wyn found that getting a job was the key to much more than a wage. Instead:

> It was a way of contributing to society through the use of one's personal skills, a means of expressing, and confirming one's gender and a means of engaging in adult practices. The wage was important to ensure a basic standard of material well-being (Wilson & Wyn 1987, p. 40).

Friendship was central to their experience of school. This included their friendships with each other, and the nature of their relationships with teachers. Frequently the students would use humour as a medium of communication, anticipating their participation in adult practices in the workplace. Although students' attempts to influence processes in the classroom through the use of humour were at times acceded to by staff, they ran the risk of being seen as merely disruptive.

Wilson and Wyn (1987) argue that these priorities are not idiosyncratic, but instead reflect more fundamental aspects of cultural formation: solidarity, informality and access to adult practices. This insight is useful in understanding the processes whereby young people leave school early. At the time of the study by Wilson and Wyn, the youth labour market had just begun to shrink, and it was becoming apparent to the students that the transition from school to work was not going to be smooth. In the 1990s, students are acutely aware that getting a job after leaving school is difficult. In their eyes, school and work are even more tenuously linked. If, in addition, young people find that they do not have good relationships with their teachers, their two main priorities are not addressed by school. It is no wonder that young people from working class neighbourhoods continue to leave school early.

Our discussion of transitions pointed out that one of the effects of a categorical concept of youth is the bracketing of young people's experiences in the present, and a focus on young people as future workers. The uni-dimensional concept of '*the* transition to adulthood' that derives from the categorical concept of youth positions young people as 'becoming', and of interest because of what or whom they may be in the future, ignoring the present reality of young people's lives. Although a 'transitions' approach is useful in identifying important processes that affect young people, the bracketing of the present is of concern because it tends to trivialise the issue of young people's *rights* and of their full *participation* in society. Young people are also citizens, not just in the future, but in the present. However, their understanding of and participation in democratic processes are seldom a priority in the institutions in which they are involved.

In understanding the transitions that young people make towards adult life, it is important to take account of the multiple layers that are involved in this process. When we explore personal dimensions of the transitions, it becomes apparent that there is a contradictory process at work. On the one hand, as many researchers have commented, the process of becoming adult has become extended over a longer time. Whereas once achieving a livelihood was possible by getting a full-time job on leaving school at age 16 or 17, and young people were able to live independently of their parents in affordable accommodation by the time they were 20, this has now become almost unheard of. Instead, getting full-time work is delayed until after a period of education and training until 19 years of age, and frequently into the early twenties, and living independently is very difficult. In her study of the processes young Australians face in becoming independent, Hartley (1989) documents these changes and their impact on young people.

On the other hand, although achieving a livelihood is deferred, other aspects of young people's lives are not. Some young people engage in 'adult practices' from a relatively early age, and perhaps they always have. By adult practices we mean that young people have responsibilities for the care of their younger siblings or parents, or to make a contribution to the family economy through their paid or unpaid work; they are involved in sexual relationships, and before they leave school, some are themselves parents. By the age of 17 the majority of Australian young people regularly use alcohol during their leisure time (Department of School Education 1992). Despite their centrality, these aspects of life are the most likely to be ignored in the curriculum, even in the senior years. It is important to recognise that young people are also citizens who are engaged in social practices in the same way as 'adults'.

Before we discuss these dimensions of young people's experiences, it is important to address the issue of the systematic amnesia on the part of educational institutions. The failure to provide a space in the crowded curriculum where young people can develop a perspective on sexual politics, labour practices and their impact on their own lives is not just an oversight. As Connell comments, what descriptions of young people's perceptions and experiences (ethnographies) cannot show 'is the institutional shape of the education system as a whole' (1994 p. 136). The failure of schools to engage with the most central issues in young people's lives is part of 'the logic of an institution embodying the power of the state and the cultural authority of the dominant class' (Connell 1994, p. 136).

It becomes much easier to understand the impact of education as a powerful institution by looking at the experiences of the very groups who tend to be systematically marginalised by it. We have already discussed some of the groups who fall into this category. Young people who are poor are amongst the most identifiable. Young people who leave school early come overwhelmingly from poor families (Lamb 1994).

Some groups of young women are also marginalised through schooling. Although young women now outnumber young men in the senior years of secondary schooling, their participation remains within a narrower range of the curriculum, reflected in their educational and occupational segregation in a narrow range of post-compulsory options (Teese et al. 1993) and in the labour market. These outcomes are really the effects of the institutionalised and systematic failure of educational institutions to address the central issues of becoming adult for many young women and for young people who are poor.

For young women, growing up means having to negotiate their sexuality and gender identity in a culture in which adult female sexuality and femininity are regarded with ambivalence. Davies (1993) offers a challenging assessment of the negotiation of feminine identities for young women in Australia. The different groups of girls she describes have different ways of constructing their femininity in relation to masculinity (related to their class location). Although each of the visions of femininity these girls portray includes a sense of themselves as powerful, Davies concludes:

> The powerful visions or images that the girls have of themselves are broken up. Like the wind blowing on the puddle of water, the words they speak involve exclusion, difference, violence. These words, and the knowledge of the social structures which discriminate against women break up the powerful images seen so clearly and with such pleasure (Davies 1993, pp. 87–8).

In addition, young women have to work out the broader implications of achieving a livelihood. This means coming to an understanding about the relationship between paid and unpaid labour, and the meaning of work itself as a place where relationships with others are forged. The meaning of work as an aspect of identity is central to understanding the outcomes for young women.

The girls in Davies' study mostly saw themselves as being able to get jobs as good as their male counterparts'. Some were very aware of the importance of being able to achieve economic independence. Despite this, the futures they envisaged already contained the knowledge of serious contradictions—although they were not necessarily seen as such. For example, the 'eastern public girls' felt that they could achieve anything 'without compromising the integrity of their relations with the children they might have in the future' (Davies 1993, p. 87). However, at the same time, they also talked about 'falling in love' and the partial curtailment of their freedom that this would involve.

The main issues which these girls were trying to work out are those associated with the social practices of being adult women in a rapidly changing world. The young people in the study by Wilson and Wyn (1987) were also fundamentally concerned with learning about and engaging with the types of social practices that they thought would be the basis of their adult lives. The issue of social practices has recently been raised by Connell in his discussion of education and poverty. In arguing for the need to change to a curriculum that addresses the real needs of all young people, he calls for 'a broader conception of educational effects as the development of capacities for social practice' (1994, p. 141). The social practices addressed by schooling, he argues, would include the winning of a livelihood, the construction of gender and the negotiation of sexuality, and the mobilisation of social power. These social practices reflect the concerns of young people, especially those for whom the process of growing up is ignored by the schooling system.

Growing up involves young people in the process of constructing identities in the context of their family life, geographical location and social location. Identities are constructed through social practices that are gendered and classed; they are personal, but also fundamentally social, shaped by the practices of institutions. The process of growing up, then, involves young people, from the earliest age, in the processes of social division in which all young people are located differently, and in which inequalities and disadvantage as well as privilege are central.

The research on young people who are systematically marginalised through the main institutions (and especially through schools) reveals that one of the most important issues is the capacity to understand one's positioning, and the development of the capacity to negotiate the social practices of gender relations, of gaining a livelihood and of sexuality. Each of these social practices involves relations of power, in which individuals are positioned because of their social location. For example, a young woman growing up in a wealthy family in the country will be engaging with very different social practices from those a young Aboriginal man living in poverty on the fringe of a large urban area engages with. Both will, at times, face the 'exclusion, difference and violence' that are the expression of institutionalised practices of social division. The issue is learning how to mobilise the social power that is available to each group.

Our discussion of social practices has pointed out that traditionally the transition to adulthood has been seen as an individual issue, focusing on young people as the potential bearers of skills to 'make something of themselves'. Taking an approach which places the *development of social practices* at its centre, by contrast, exposes the power relations that are an integral part of the process of growing up. Young people are engaging with powerful institutional processes as they develop their identities, their perspectives on life and as they create the spaces within which they can participate in society.

CONCLUSION

Becoming adult is now widely acknowledged to be a process which includes multiple dimensions. It is also increasingly recognised that it is not easy to 'mark' the points of arrival at adult status. Nonetheless, the concept of youth transitions has tended to remain locked into a linear and relatively uni-dimensional notion of growing up, especially in the policies that inform education and training.

Taking the example of early school-leavers in Australia, our discussion has focused attention on the ways in which the institution of schooling systematically marginalises some groups of young people. The institutionalised processes which dominate the processes of growing up are different from country to country. In each of the cases discussed above, however, the 'transition processes' that are structured by institutions can be seen to be failing to offer real pathways for all young people towards a livelihood. Achieving a livelihood has historically been a struggle. What we are witnessing in the resurgence of interest in transitions in the 1990s, across almost all societies, is the increasing divisions between those for whom livelihood is achievable and those who become systematically marginalised.

In this chapter we have explored one of the central issues—the disjuncture between education and employment for increasing numbers of young people. Clearly, one of the questions this raises, in each of the cases we have discussed, is to what extent does schooling really include all groups of young people? However, there is a further issue for young people which goes beyond schooling. Young people are marginalised by education and training, but the significance of being marginalised in this way is framed by the failure of labour markets to provide employment. In the next chapter we discuss youth marginalisation in its broadest context.

6   Youth marginalisation

One consequence of the social processes we have described in this book is that often young people do not have the power to shape their lives as they might otherwise have done. Specific case studies and ethnographies of young people do illustrate the many and varied ways in which young people are presently 'making sense' of their world and how they are actively constructing their own life patterns and experiences. Yet when all is said and done, the issues surrounding youth identity and youth 'agency' are ultimately circumscribed, and contextualised, by the dominant social relations within which young people are positioned.

A major point of this chapter, in fact, is that in order to understand the central issues facing young people it is necessary to move beyond a focus on young people themselves, to the changing relationship between different groups of young people and society in its broadest sense. Focusing on the *processes* of marginalisation offers a way of grasping the systematic nature of the exclusion of some groups of young people from full participation in society and its institutions. We argue that although some young people who are 'marginalised' will find ways of establishing a legitimate livelihood in time, as they have in previous times, circumstances have changed, altering the significance of marginalisation. Changing economic, social and political conditions of the 1990s mean that we cannot assume that once excluded full participation in society is just a matter of 'growing up'. Rethinking youth means rethinking the very role that young people have in society, and the responsibilities that society has for youth.

This chapter outlines the processes of marginalisation as an effect of social division. 'Marginalisation' is a term used to describe aspects of life experiences through which inequality is structured. The chapter considers recent changes and shifts in the nature of social welfare provision. We argue that one consequence of these changes is the emergence of a discourse which sees the marginalised as part of an 'underclass'. The ideological significance of the notion of 'underclass' is explored by considering the issues of state intervention and citizenship rights. The chapter concludes with a discussion of how young people themselves are responding to economic pressures and state interventions.

ON THE MARGINS

Young people do not form a uniform or homogenous social group. As pointed out by Graycar and Jamrozik (1989), for example, major class- and gender-based differences exist with regard to housing, family relationships, education, the labour market, and cultural activity. To live in an affluent suburb, to succeed at school and continue on to tertiary study, to move into some kind of professional employment—these are still the trajectories of the sons and daughters of the wealthy. These selfsame young people are also the targets for aggressive 'youth' marketing campaigns, as potential and actual buyers of the latest designer clothes, 'labels' and music.

While there are still clear 'winners' today, it is the majority of working people who pay for the privileges of the rich and their offspring to enjoy life to the fullest. For the rest, it is hard work accommodating to or resisting the stresses and strains of the economic rationalist agenda. And, for some, it is a time of loss, and to be a 'loser'. The pressures on the working are sustained largely by the pressures on those who are not working.

The people who are placed on the margins are those who by and large come from the poorest housing estates and suburbs. They have limited means, and small incomes, and often share subsistence living with others in similar conditions. They are compelled to sell their labour in return for a wage—but are disadvantaged in doing so by institutional processes which force them out of education early, and which deny them the skills and credentials to compete on the private labour market. Some idea of the despair and frustration of young people in such low-income neighbourhoods is indicated in the following quotations:

> It's not a working class area—there's no work whatsoever in [name of suburb] (CA 123 in White 1995).

... a lot of people are real fussy who they employ now ... a few of my mates have gone for jobs 'n they've sorta asked for qualifications 'n experience, but how can you have experience when ya, you know, they ask for 19 year olds or 18 year olds 'n you've only been in the workforce two minutes so how can you have experience (CA 135 in White 1995).

The actual experiences of life on the margins are the continuing source of much anger and anxiety on the part of those young people so marginalised. Even where some kind of paid work can be found, the treatment of many young people by employers, for example, can exacerbate the difficulties of economic hardship in a number of ways:

I was an apprentice like you're on the minimum wage as it is and what made it even worse was like he wasn't paying me and like I always had to lend money off my girlfriend, off my parents, and like when I did get my pay it all went to paying people back (CA 131 in White 1995).

Cos younger people get a lower, a minimum wage, it's, most of the work around here is part-time and it's really not worth working you know cos like you get it, what it is, seven dollars an hour and then you get taxed on it and then at the end of the week you know, you're working a few hours a week part-time and you get more money on the dole ... so there's no use in working part-time so the only work you can get is worth getting is full-time work (CA 115 in White 1995).

There's not a real lot of places that set out to employ young people, there's really no-one except for the fast food chains and they only want you cause you're a cheap labour. They're just using you as soon as you're too old they'll get rid of ya, they'll find a problem with ya (CA 119 in White 1995).

As discussed in chapter two, the closing off of opportunities in the formal wage economy, coupled with the low wages available for part-time work, has created pressures on young working class people to adopt creative methods of gaining a livelihood, including such things as finding cash-in-hand work, and engaging in criminal activity. These are hardly preferable alternatives to meaningful, well-paid work. Nor should they be romanticised into something they are not:

Cash-in-hand questions stink because you don't know if you are getting award wages sort of thing. I mean they give you $3 an hour and it's cash-in-hand and you can't do anything about it because you don't want to go through the tax department and get the tax taken away (SA 128 in White 1995).

Most of the people I know who deal drugs don't actually use them themselves. Like now I know people who do use the drugs but a lot of the people doing it now are only doing it for the money. Like I know people who do it to pay for their rent and stuff so they just have to (SA 113 in White 1995).

I don't know why you'd do it if there's no money in it. I'd only do a crime if there's something in it. It's stupid to do it in the first place. They get bored. There's shit all to do these days. There's nothing to do at all. You sit around at home and all you do is think about what to do and then if something comes up, you give it a try and it works, it's a good rush, then you do it again (SA 123 in White 1995).

Life on the margins is difficult financially. It is difficult from the point of view of making ends meet, and from achieving the status of 'worth' as a human being in a wage-based capitalist economy. It can be very boring. And even one's consumption habits can lead to problems. This is especially so if there are existing prejudices and visible markers of difference which predispose certain types of intervention:

There's about 30 of us, mostly Koories [Aborigines]. When we hang out in [entertainment complex], they told me we can't hang out there at night any more because people are too scared to walk in there. He said the police are going to come down and stop us hanging around. But it's their business they're losing. We spend about $30 each in there when we've got money (DA 163 in White 1995).

Whether it be school, work or the street, the same categories and groups of young people are marginal. It is young people in working class communities, in some societies it is blacks, indigenous people and people from other than English speaking backgrounds. The marginalised have in common a general position of relative powerlessness in society and shared experiences of social division which are exacerbated through the operation of mainstream social institutions such as schools. Life on the margins is made, it is not a 'natural' phenomenon.

PROCESSES OF MARGINALISATION

So what precisely is marginalisation? Some groups of young people are in increasing numbers being disenfranchised from the major institutions and material benefits of consumer society. In particular, they are being subjected to the dual processes of *disconnection* from institutions revolving around production, consumption and community life, and the social and psychological experiences of *disempowerment* accompanying this disconnection.

Social disconnection from the institutions of work, school and family is evident in the practices associated with production, consumption and reproduction. For example, in the sphere of *production*, the impact of industrial restructuring in advanced industrial countries has been to replace full-time jobs, which offered opportunities for on-the-job training and some notion of career for young people, with part-time jobs which go nowhere. Given this structure, many young people are forced to exist 'on the margins' of production, earning barely enough to sustain a legitimate livelihood, or exist on unemployment benefits.

One of the implications of these practices in the sphere of production is that this marginalised group of young people are also excluded from mainstream consumer activity. Their patterns of *consumption* reflect their marginal status. As Jones and Wallace (1992) point out in their discussion of young people as consumer citizens, in the area of consumption as in other areas of young people's lives, there are contradictory tendencies. Thus, on the one hand, as we have identified, one of the most significant issues about youth is that many have little access to an income, and many suffer extreme poverty. Against this reality, buoyant consumer markets offer the prospect of power, identity and independence to all young people (see also Johnson 1993). These circumstances place some young people in a contradictory situation. There is increasing *divergence* in young people's experience between the products that are available for consumption by them, which on the surface appears to be 'inclusive', and the reality of exclusion from expected standards of living (Jones & Wallace 1992, pp. 137–8). The contradiction is also that although young people share cultural symbols and language derived from the media, they certainly do not share the means to buy the consumer goods which accompany these symbols.

In the sphere of *reproduction*, the increasing dependence on parents means that the process of establishing their own space for relationships is drawn out. While some young people do not mind living at home for an extended period, it is not possible or suitable for many. Young men tend to stay at home longer than young women (Hartley 1989). While unemployment may slow down the process of family formation for men, it speeds up the process for women (Jones & Wallace 1992). In the literature, especially from Britain, discussion has focused around the process of 'leaving home', a process which has become polarised: for one group of young people staying on in the parental home presents few problems; for another group, the delay in being able to establish their own more independent space is a significant issue (Heath 1995).

Table 6.1 Dimensions of lived experience

	Positive	Negative	Contingent
Time	Productive; focused; combines necessity & choice	Endless; bunched	Spare time; irregular
Space	Legitimacy in use; privacy; access to transport	Outsider status; strict regulation; limited mobility	Own territory; earned sanctuary
Activity	Worthwhile; lead to reward; combines necessity and choice	Meaningless; false 'busyness'	Choices in doing nothing; creative
Resources	Regular income; access to health & education, etc.; primary sources	Bare survival; irregular; multiple sources	In exchange for something; dependency
Identity	Self-confidence; social connection; future planning	Low confidence; social disconnection; day-to-day existence	Subcultures; alternative communities

Young people experience these processes of exclusion and marginalisation in very immediate and personal ways. Table 7.1 illustrates the impact of marginalisation at the concrete level of lived experience. Positive life experiences tend to be associated with a more mainstream status, particularly with regard to secure income and employment prospects. Negative experiences are linked to economic, social and political marginalisation, which in turn directly affect how young people engage in and with time, space, activity, resources and identity formation. Experience is not reducible to simply positive and negative categories. This is recognised in the idea that much of human life is contingent—that is, how we respond to events and social capacities also depends upon both the specific circumstances of an individual (or group), and the degree of self-conscious 'human agency' in choosing to act and react to these circumstances in particular ways.

The point of the table, however, is to draw attention to the fact that the prior structural allocation of societal resources has a profound effect on how young people actually live their lives. This resource allocation thus sets up the broad parameters within which activity, including identity formation, occurs.

THE STRUCTURING OF INEQUALITIES

At the level of broad generalisation, economic inequality is not necessarily contingent upon a 'closed circle' of social allocation and decision-making, in which the same select few are granted certain privileges exclusively on the basis of who they are. For instance, and particularly in most advanced industrialised countries today, there is no formal exclusion of people based upon ascriptive criteria such as sex, age or ethnic background. Theoretically, what counts in the present era is 'what a person does', and how they marshal their capabilities and personal will to further their own economic prospects. In practical terms, however, we know that the major social tendency is for intergenerational class, gender and ethnic patterns of inequality to continue and, more recently, to become even more entrenched and polarised.

Studies of the perspectives of young people provide an insight into the way in which young people actively 'marginalise' themselves. For example, it is rarely necessary to actively exclude young women from areas of the labour market, because they often exclude themselves. There are many studies which reveal the limited career aspirations of girls and young women. On the other hand, there are also studies of labour processes which reveal the ways in which changing workplace practices nonetheless retain processes which exclude or marginalise women. Probert and Wilson's (1993) collection of essays called *Pink Collar Blues*, for example, provides many examples of the gendered nature of work practices in areas where new technology is being introduced.

Other studies provide examples of the ways in which some groups of young people marginalise themselves from mainstream schooling. A recent Australian study demonstrated that working class girls were not anti-school, they simply objected to the fact that their teachers were not taking them seriously and were spending most of their time with the 'posh' girls (Walker 1993). The working class girls were seen as undisciplined, precisely because their behaviour reflected the lack of assistance and attention provided by their teachers. What this study illustrates, importantly, is the strength of cultural perspectives and the role these have in the negotiation of institutional practices.

A third area where young people might be seen to actively marginalise themselves is that of juvenile justice. Once again the dialectical connection between experience, choice and institutional structures is essential to consider, if we are to adequately interpret the actions of young people. For instance, young people may choose to adopt certain youth culture styles as a way to express themselves. Each particular choice of 'style', however, carries with it certain implications with respect to how others will respond to the young person. The police, for example, tend to perceive groups of young people as being a problem, or not a problem, according to their youth culture style. The issue of whether necessity or choice is behind a particular street-level display is also important to consider in this context. As pointed out by Sercombe (1993), choosing to be a punk or skinhead (that is, a member of spectacular youth subculture) is very different from being forced to be a street dweller (that is, to join the ranks of the homeless). In either case, the relationship between a particular group and state officials such as police or social workers has important implications in terms of perceptions and institutional reinforcements of marginal status.

There are instances as well where choosing to be 'marginal' in one system or society is an important part of establishing one's identity and status in another network of relationships. As part of the work of the Royal Commission into Aboriginal Deaths in Custody, for example, it was discovered that many young indigenous people in Australia view incarceration as more of an 'abode' than outside home life, and in some cases prison may inadvertently become a symbol of status. Imprisonment thus is seen as a means of establishing credibility among some young Aborigines who, the report says, might be described as 'street kids' (Johnston 1991, p. 168). Here we have a case where the young people themselves are the apparent instigators and inventors of new traditions of marginalisation. But once again, to view such choices as indications of a meaningful or positive 'agency' is to take such actions out of their historical and institutional context, particularly with respect to the relationship between indigenous young people and the police (see, for example, Cunneen 1994).

It is important to acknowledge different types of inequality and poverty as well, particularly as these are related to life-cycle processes. For example, young people from affluent families may, technically speaking, be 'poor' relative to adults in their sphere of relations. Likewise, they may go through a transitional period, such as being a student at university, where they are 'poor' in terms of material possessions and financial resources. Such 'poverty' is, however, purely transient in nature, and may occasionally be seen as part of the normal, toughing it out type of 'coming of age' process associated with more affluent strata of the population. In contrast, for many young people from low-income backgrounds poverty is neither 'character-building' nor simply a stage—it is both background and a permanent condition. It is thus necessary to distinguish between temporary versus enduring patterns of poverty.

The evidence on worldwide distribution of wealth and poverty points to a major polarisation of wealth and income on the one hand and poverty levels on the other. This is occurring both on a regional basis (that is, across the north–south divide) and within the advanced capitalist countries. Levels of youth unemployment, poverty and homelessness are high virtually everywhere on the globe (United Nations 1993) including the industrialised countries where, with few exceptions, there has been a tendency for youth unemployment to grow, for the duration of youth unemployment to lengthen, and for a proliferation of training and education programs to soak up as many of the unemployed as possible until some unspecified future 'recovery'. The pitfalls and realities of this stage of late capitalism are especially apparent in the case of newcomers to the global market society, as witnessed by the large and rapidly growing unemployment queues in Russia and now China.

The prevalence of social polarisation is also evident in the urban structuring of inequality in cities such as New York, London, Berlin and Sydney. Here, increasingly, we are seeing the visual confirmations of such poverty in congregations of 'street people', including the homeless, the beggar, the vagabond, the hangabout. Young people constitute a sizeable proportion of street-present non-consumers, and as we shall see, have become the principal target of many campaigns designed to restore the street to 'respectability' and 'safety'.

Acknowledgement must be made as well of the historical con- struction and persistence of racism which brutally marginalises people. The dynamics of racism vary depending upon national context. Thus, the dispossession of indigenous people in North America and Australasia is quite a different matter from the impo- sition of a slave-based economy in the southern United States, which in turn is different from racism accompanying the movement of transient 'guest' workers within the Africa–Europe or Mexico–United States nexus. The position of certain select communities at the bottom of the social pyramid is subject to ongoing contestation, and contin- ual policy debate about and state responses to 'underclass' conditions. Certainly the life prospects of indigenous young people in Canada, the United States and Australia are immediately affected by the colonial legacy and the racism, stereotyping, lack of adequate resourcing and state social control linked to post-colonial rule.

The hierarchical ordering of different immigrant communities and indigenous people, relative to the holders of power and wealth generally, is a major issue incorporating many dimensions (Guerra & White 1995). For example, the migrant community in Australia is extensive and incredibly diverse. With over 100 cultural and national groups represented, Australia is one of the most polyethnic countries in the world. Yet, as sociological research continues to affirm, the country's power structures continue to remain largely monocultural and with particular groups. Certain categories of non- English speaking background migrants are more disadvantaged than others at an institutional level in terms of gaining benefits, services, and paid work (see Collins 1988; Castles et al. 1988; Jamrozik et al. 1995).

Interestingly, the young people most likely to leave school early today in Australia are not the children of the immigrants of the 1950s to 1970s, but instead, the children of the more established, English speaking working class. Children from non-English speaking backgrounds in Australia have achieved relatively highly in education during the 1980s and 1990s (Lamb 1994). Given the recurrent series of recessions over the last two decades, however, the levels of unemployment in the post-1976 immigrant communities has been extremely high.

It is important to recognise how the processes of marginalisation operate with respect to particular cultural groups. Each cultural group faces particular issues. Muslim students, for example, face serious contradictions in their education in all secular societies, the resolution of which is almost impossible, and the result of which is often the marginalisation of these students from the education system as they leave school early. The separation of religion and state is a crucial issue for Muslim parents seeking to educate their children:

> the public education system ensures the separation of church and state, a pivotal element of the American way of life. To those from Islamic cultures, such a separation is perplexing at best and unthinkable at worst. In an education system, this separation is seen as having a number of deleterious effects (Pulcini 1990, p. 128).

One of the contradictions faced by Muslim youth in schooling is that although formally based on a separation of religion and state, in most advanced industrialised countries, such as Australia, the school system is actually underpinned by Judeo-Christian values, which constitute an important part of the hegemonic curriculum. In providing a culturally sensitive environment for young Muslim people, teachers need to be careful not to put Muslim students in situations that violate their religion, for example, by eating pork and other unlawful foods, or by forcing female students to participate in physical education classes where they would have to expose their bodies. Hicks and Moh'd (1995) provide examples of how a school at Port Hedland has approached these issues to include Muslim students more fully in schooling. To the extent that this inclusive approach is ignored by teachers and other members of the community, it actively marginalises young people by excluding them, at the same time making the process of exclusion seem invisible.

Finally, and crucially, the proliferation of political, war and economic refugees in recent years must be considered in any contemporary discussion of marginalisation. The majority of the world's

refugees are women, children and young people. The special difficulties faced by refugee young people needs to be highlighted. These
young people often face multiple difficulties in negotiating the transitions towards adult life in their new country. In a similar vein,
refugees or immigrants from war-torn countries—such as the Leba-
nese, Vietnamese and Cambodians—are likely to have their schooling
interrupted, and thus to have very low levels of post-school qualifications (Moss 1993).

SOCIAL WELFARE PROVISION

Social welfare provision is one of the central mechanisms for ensuring
that young people are not so marginalised that they feel they do not
even belong to society. While it is a truism that the rich have got
richer, the gap between rich and poor is also now due to the fact
that in many cases the poor are getting poorer too. Thus the
disparities between rich and poor, and the extent of poverty, have
grown in both the first and the third worlds. As Durning (1990,
p. 135) graphically puts it:

> In 1989, the world had 157 billionaires, perhaps 2 million million-
> aires, and 100 million homeless. Americans spend $5 billion each
> year on special diets to lower their calorie consumption, while 400
> million people around the world are so undernourished their bodies
> and minds are deteriorating.

In the light of such gross discrepancies in wealth, it is reasonable
to ask what kind of public or state support exists for those who
have been shut out of the economic affluence.

Here it is important to consider the nature of transformations
occurring with respect to the 'welfare state' and welfare provision
generally. In each of the advanced capitalist countries we have seen
a very similar shift in the broad functions and benefit provisions of
the welfare apparatus of the state. This is particularly evident in
countries such as Britain, New Zealand, Australia and even Sweden,
which have long had well-established and extensive welfare apparatus. The 'fiscal crisis of the state' has translated at a practical policy
level into conscious decisions by governments (of both 'conservative'
and 'social democratic' political traditions) to deal in particular ways
with the tension between assisting capital accumulation and accommodating poverty and need.

Under the guiding ideology and rhetoric of economic rationalism,
governments have basically moved to reduce spending (relative to
need) in the area of social welfare, while state subsidies and 'welfare'
provision for the corporate sector (for example through tax cuts and

financial incentive schemes) have not only continued but have been stepped up. Furthermore, the tax burden has been systematically shifted away from the rich and the corporate sector, and placed squarely on the backs of the pay-as-you-earn wage worker. The outcome of such measures has been a steady dismantling of the welfare apparatus of the state, as manifest for instance in concerted movements towards ever more selective rather than universal systems of benefits and services. Related to this, the corporatisation and privatisation of formerly non-capitalist state enterprises, such as health, public transport and education, are being accomplished in ways which have major social implications for the target user groups, but according to the goals of 'economic efficiency' and user pays models of service provision.

The decreasing availability and quality of public services, coupled with the low level of benefit payment, can be analysed from the specific vantage point of young people's requirements and financial resources. On the one hand, it is clearly the case that economically young people do indeed have 'adult' needs when it comes to items such as housing, food, clothing and everyday maintenance. Furthermore, however, they often have living costs associated with education, training and work, such as transport, books, special fees and so on. Evidence consistently points to the fact that young people who are reliant upon state support for physical survival and/or engagement in developmental activities such as education are effectively forced to rely on payments well below the poverty line (Hartley & Wolcott 1994).

The rolling back of the welfare apparatus of the state is not only evident in the specific area of 'social welfare'; it is also linked to broad spending cutbacks or rationalisation processes in public transportation, public housing, and education and training. Across the industrialised world, while school student numbers have increased, governments have been increasingly reticent to put money into developing the infrastructure of a quality education for all school students. Social class differences in educational provision have in many cases sharpened, due to the impact of differential systems competing with each other (for example, private versus state provision), skewed patterns of government spending for particular school sectors (for example, declines in public provision and increases for the private schools), and the closure of state schools with improper planning.

The economic rationalist agenda in education has been accompanied by pressures to amalgamate schools, increase class sizes, reduce curricular offerings and to demand even more from already stretched teaching staff. Education, and students, are increasingly being treated simply as 'commodities', something to be bought and sold on the 'market'. The pervasiveness of such thinking, and the adoption of corporate management models and the commercialisation of schooling have had a significant impact upon the social and pedagogical processes, content and structures of education. Much the same can be said about 'training' in its many and varied forms. In other words, the restructuring of developmental social institutions in line with the requirements and demands of contemporary capitalist accumulation is radically altering their historical role in society. In doing so, they are also altering the historical role of young people in society.

Education and training now play a significant role as 'holding tanks' for the young unemployed. This is apparent in the significance now given to apparent retention rates by educational policy (for example, Finn 1991) and the assumptions made in educational policy about the need for further education and training. This is also apparent in the ways in which 'welfare' provision per se is invariably tied to an education or training agenda. To understand the nexus between welfare provision and such developmental activities, it is useful to explore the relationship between welfare and unemployment and how this is generally conceptualised.

The development of social institutions such as the school, and of social welfare, are historically linked to the changes and demands of the capitalist labour market. The preparation of future workers and home-carers—ideologically, functionally and socially—has been a crucial aspect of the social reproduction role of the school. Meanwhile, the role of social welfare, as broadly conceived, has been to provide residual protection to those people who have for some reason been excluded from the waged labour market. In most industrialised countries, social welfare has thus been an 'add-on' to the capitalist market, rather than integral to state planning and coordination. The provision of 'welfare' can be seen to be both generated by capitalism (via the market which broadly sets the level of employment and compensation for labour) and structured by the needs of capital in terms of its share of state resources and tax benefits (via fiscal, monetary and wages policy).

If we exclude direct and indirect concessions made to the more affluent and the business sector, and if we exclude institutions such as schools, then welfare provision can, in effect, be reduced to providing income support for people who are out of work. Distinctions can be made here between different categories of 'the poor', the 'unemployed' and 'welfare beneficiaries', and where young people tend to fit within each of these socially constructed categories in terms of perceived 'responsibilities' and 'capacities'. For example, the so called 'impotent poor' are those young people who are seen to not be responsible for their unemployment, and who are defined by their incapacity or diminished capacity to work (for example, people with intellectual and/or physical disabilities, the chronically ill).

On the other hand, there are those welfare recipients who do have full capacity, but not the opportunity, to engage in paid work. This category includes the majority of those young people reliant upon state welfare benefits and services as the primary source of subsistence. These young people are seen to be more responsible for their own welfare and work prospects and called on to demonstrate to the state that they are indeed exercising their capacities correctly in the pursuit of paid work. Programs and benefits may be differentiated according to the length of time one is outside the formal labour force (for example, short-term and long-term unemployment programs). The overall orientation, however, is for state welfare to be tied to structured 'pathways' which facilitate skill development, motivation and ready insertion into the paid labour force. In this way, the individual is held responsible to take advantage of any training or education program on offer, and to demonstrate concretely that they are trying to find work in a diligent fashion.

The content of welfare provision, and the organisational structure within which it takes place, are not neutral. Programs which link benefits to participation are not merely concerned to meet the individual needs of the welfare recipient. In many cases, as has been ably documented in various national contexts (for example, Finn 1987; White 1990; Beasley 1991), such programs are intended to provide a fairly narrow kind of work preparation, one which emphasises the work ethic, compliant attitudes and behaviour, and constant 'busyness' in terms of everyday activities. The targets of such welfare provision are basically meant to comply with the dictates of the welfare provider with regard to how they organise their lives and their daily routines.

Institutional arrangements which are designed to control and modify public and private behaviour have been described via use of the concept of 'governmentality'. This refers to the ways in which institutional regimes, knowledges, practices and procedures are structured so as to exercise power over and through certain populations. According to Rose (1989), childhood is the most intensely governed part of personal existence. Governmentality is carried out through education, child welfare and juvenile justice institutions and personnel, and is concerned ultimately with the management and regulation of 'the self' in contemporary society.

A critical evaluation of recent trends in welfare provision suggests that we are witnessing a period of intense scrutiny of the private and public lives of young people. Many interventions designed to 'help' young people (for example, to get a job) embody strategies which are consciously designed to discipline young people 'from the inside out'. That is, the push is to get young people themselves to 'take responsibility' for their appearance, their language, their manners, their own public self-image and public performance in a way which leaves little room for deviation from what is deemed to be 'normal'. It is up to the young person to censor themselves, to develop their own regime of self-discipline and self-control.

Institutionally, the shift towards such things as 'case management' approaches across the welfare and justice domains has a number of implications as well for how state and non-government workers perceive young people (for example, as 'clients', as 'rights holders'), and how they might work with, for or even against certain young people (for example, as 'experts', as 'advocates'). It is important to acknowledge here that while the overall orientation of the institutions of the welfare apparatus of the state is informed by a 'control' agenda, the same cannot be said of those who actually people these institutions. In other words, just as we must acknowledge that young people can and do resist the various manifestations of governmentality, so too workers with youth likewise have different ideological and political agendas, some of which may run counter to the broad institutional patterns.

CRIMINALISING THE UNEMPLOYED

Restrictive and intrusive welfare provision can be experienced as especially negative by many young people. The processes of poverty alleviation can, in effect, create both the conditions for the emergence of a long-term structurally marginalised population, and the 'need' for repressive state responses designed to keep this population in check.

State intervention in the lives of young people is extensive (through a wide range of welfare, education and criminal justice institutions); intensive (through increasingly intrusive measures designed to control youth activity); and contingent (through use of a range of positive and negative incentives to guide youth behaviour). Mechanisms of both 'consent' and 'coercion' are utilised to maintain social order, and these are manifest at both the level of process (for example, coercion in the form of compulsory schooling in the educational sphere) and institution (for example, criminal justice which is primarily an institution of coercion, or education which is one of developmental opportunity within which one can find positive benefit as well as negative experiences).

The resources available to, and the structuring of the social content of, institutions such as education, welfare and criminal justice have major implications for youth livelihood and their future social prospects. The broad tendency in much social policy has been to stress individual responsibility on the part of young people across these institutional contexts. For example, recent years have seen a major shift in juvenile justice from the so called 'welfare' model to the 'justice' model. Both models have essentially informed the social control of working class young people, but the latter has had an overt focus and rationale based on personal choices and responsibilities of the offender (Cunneen & White 1995). In a similar vein, much of the trend in the area of vocational education, and the link between welfare and training, has been premised upon the idea of taking personal responsibility for one's employment prospects. The shift here has been from government concern with unemployment to embracing the concept of unemployability. The characteristics of the unemployed person are thus elevated to become the target and central policy thrust of state strategic planning.

Institutional changes of this nature have had a profound impact on young people. For some young people the hurdles accompanying the provision of inadequate benefits and allowances, or attendance at institutions and programs which offer little immediate satisfaction or real enhancement of job prospects, are too high for the expected payoff. Further to this, the experience of long-term unemployment has a number of psychological consequences, not least of which is the entrenchment of feelings of inadequacy and powerlessness. The combination of a vulnerable emotional and social status, and frustration with and lack of tangible reward or personal opportunity via the social institutions, can lead to further disengagement from mainstream social life. Concretely, this can manifest itself in homelessness, suicide, illegal and criminal activity, and adoption of various alternative lifestyles.

The problems experienced by the most marginalised strata of the working class, however, are all too often responded to as if the problem is the marginalised people themselves. And here it is essential to consider the ways in which marginalisation processes have been accompanied by the *criminalisation* of those sections of the population which do not come under direct surveillance and control via the welfare state. In other words, the processes of class division and polarisation are evident not only with respect to the distribution of societal resources and in the operation of mainstream social institutions; they are also apparent in the class biases ingrained in street policing and the imperatives of the criminal justice system.

At the centre of the criminalisation process is a clear social control agenda. The use of state repression against the most marginalised strata of the population is symbolically important in terms of keeping the lid on social unrest, and deflecting attention away from the structural reasons for poverty and unemployment in the first place.

It has been suggested that the demise of the 'social state' is in fact intertwined with the increasing prominence of the 'repressive state' (White 1996). As part of the justification for taking a 'tougher stance' on issues such as welfare allocation and law and order, greater attention in recent years has been given to the growth in the so called 'underclass'.

The ideological construction of the youth 'underclass' can initially be considered by juxtaposing a structural explanation, which focuses upon prior conditions of poverty and unemployment, with a behavioural perspective, which focuses upon social deviancy and antisocial tendencies within this alienated strata of young people. In more analytical terms, table 7.2 outlines the main dimensions of 'underclass' as generally discussed in media treatments and by academics. The difficulty with attempts to spell out the objective and subjective dimensions of the 'underclass' with both right wing and left wing interpretations is that too often the concept itself is granted legitimacy without adequate critical reflection on what it actually connotes. One of the problems with the term is that it can be seen to imply both a retreat from class analysis (since, by definition, the 'underclass' is outside the existing class structure) and a distancing from explanations which see the expansion of this social strata as part and parcel of wider class polarisation processes (since it is usually framed in terms of 'the poor', rather than the relationship between rich and poor).

On a different note, the use of the concept has also been criticised because of its supposed 'controlling' connotations. That is, the discourse of 'underclass' is itself seen to be implicated in a more general system of governance targeted at young people with a view to regulating their perceived potential disruptiveness. Indeed, the dangers of the discourse are such that the 'will to regulate' is seen to cut across the political divide. Thus, as Bessant (1995, p. 45) sees it, there is a 'possibility that the left and the right share certain commonalities such as the need to designate problem populations and devise strategies for their management'. Such an evaluation, however, ignores both the substantive differences between left wing and right wing commentators (as illustrated in table 7.2), and underestimates the reflective and strategic thinking which may underpin the use of the term. Most importantly, criticism and rejection of certain 'discourse' in absolutist terms—whether it be with regard to the idea of an 'underclass' or that of the 'homeless' (see Bessant 1995; Tait 1993)—itself fails to do justice to the ambiguities of language. The 'naming' of certain categories of young people in particular ways can be part of a controlling agenda. But, just as importantly, such 'naming' can be part of an emancipatory project as well, one which young people themselves may find attractive and

Table 6.2   Dimensions of 'underclass'

| Dimension | Description | Interpretation | |
		Right wing	Left wing
Subjective position	General social attitudes, values and behaviour	Personal choice & 'dependency culture'	Survivalist desperation; few choices
	Antisocial; anti-authority; disrespectful	Dangerous; immoral; irresponsible; socially deviant	Victims; brutalised; alienated
Objective position	Position in labour market/welfare	Hand-out mentality; welfare bludgers; risky lifestyle & undisciplined	Structure of paid work; structure of welfare provision
	Marginal to labour market; excluded from state welfare provision	Unwillingness to work, train or be educated	Reserve labour; surplus population

identify with, and within which they too can assert agency. The politics of 'discourse' are such that social context and concrete action objectives do shape the overall meaning and resonance of the discourse. Thus, the social meaning of terms such as 'underclass' tend to have a shifting and contingent nature.

Regardless of definitional problems or conceptual debates, the ideological power of the concept is nevertheless manifest in day-to-day discourse. In particular, it is usually linked with the idea of threats by 'them' against 'us'. In this sense, the very notion of an 'underclass' feeds into and is drawn from new right law and order discourse. Politically, this kind of discourse has connections with what has been called 'authoritarian populism'. Practically, this means that public concern is directed at how best to control the 'underclass', rather than with how best to eradicate the conditions from which the empirical realities arise. As Williamson argues:

> The 'underclass' is a convenient ideological tool for either abandoning any commitment to the poor and disadvantaged, or cultivating popular support for more coercive measures. The irony, in our view, is that either of these measures is in fact likely to create and solidify an underclass. It becomes a self-fulfilling prophecy. Only by developing policy approaches based on debate and broad consensus which maintain the 'permeable boundaries' between the labour market and those outside it (and indeed, between the training market and those

in status zer0) will some sense of social integration be sustained and dangerous forms of social exclusion—whether termed an 'underclass' or something else—forestalled (1995, pp. 14–15).

Williamson employs the term 'status zer0' to describe young people who are aged 16 and 17 and are not in education, training or employment. He describes the seemingly 'hopeless' situation of this group, but at the same time emphasises that 'most still subscribe to dominant *goals*, but either don't know how to get there, think it is impossible to get there or are exploring different ways of getting there' (Williamson 1995, p. 12). It is this potential for young people to participate that is often lost in the popular use of the term 'underclass'.

In this context, it needs to be emphasised that the media terms used to describe aspects of the 'underclass' are especially resonant of youth—the images are those of people who have a total lack of self-control, who engage in violent crime, who are lazy and unmotivated, and who are disrespectful of the symbols and institutions of mainstream society. The media construction of youth 'crime waves' and their 'moral panics' over youth behaviour are symptomatic of wider attempts to stigmatise and control the new 'dangerous classes' of late capitalism, the members of which are overwhelmingly young and on the margins. The images of disorder do have some grounding in material conditions and processes. That is, the plight of young people has to be considered in the light of increasing class polarisation, the growth of the 'informal' economic sector and the desperations associated with economic subsistence in highly restrictive circumstances.

REPRESSIVE STATE INTERVENTION

A politics which is based upon social exclusion (of the poor, the dispossessed, the marginalised), and which is ingrained in recent institutional changes in process and content, must have particular definite programmatic outcomes. Here it can be argued that what we are seeing in most advanced capitalist countries is the *forfeiture of basic citizen rights* for an increasing proportion of the youth population. Citizenship is increasingly contingent upon labour market position, and what 'rights' and 'claims' one can make is dependent in practice upon whether or not they are connected in some way to educational or labour market institutions.

The claim a young person makes for income support and basic services is contingent upon giving up certain rights and freedoms in return. Particularly in the area of social welfare, the unemployed are no longer entitled to state or public support—there are strings attached, obligations to fulfil and screenings to undertake. The onus is for the unemployed person to accept the multitude of work, income, asset, lifestyle and 'attitude' tests required to establish eligibility and level of state welfare support. Indeed, much welfare provision today involves an implicit criminalisation of the target population. That is, recipients are subject to increasing scrutiny by the repressive side of the welfare apparatus due to pressures to reduce the overall welfare bill. In cases such as the sole-parent benefit in Australia, it is actually assumed that the recipient is 'guilty' until proven 'innocent', insofar as they have to demonstrate their solitary status before benefit will be provided. As mentioned above, the claiming of unemployment benefits likewise involves a series of hurdles, including the demonstration of enthusiasm for job searching and re-training, and subservience to conformity (in appearance and behaviour) as dictated by welfare officials, as a condition of income support.

The lack of basic citizenship rights lies not only in the areas of welfare benefits and services, and inequalities in educational provision, it is also and perhaps most apparent in the area of criminal justice. The visibility and presence of young people in the public domains of the streets, shopping centres and malls, particularly the more marginalised, non-consuming individuals, has been met by concerted attempts to exclude or regulate them. The police, private security firms, shopping centre security staff, transit police and welfare officials are significant players with varying powers in the policing of young people's behaviour and movements (see White & Alder 1994). Importantly, young people do not have to have broken the law or engaged in actual offensive behaviour before they are subject to intrusive intervention into their affairs.

Inequality is a lived experience, and is associated with different uses of 'public' space by different groups of people. Increasingly the regulation and control of public space has focused on the young in a manner which suggests a new form of *spatial apartheid*. In effect, the social and physical space of young people 'on the margins' has been eroded and is now subject to persistent state interventions, such as campaigns to 'clean up the streets'. Young people are not considered as legitimate 'rights holders' when it comes to use of the public domain. Furthermore, state programs such as 'safer city projects' and 'community crime prevention' more often than not construct young people as 'the enemy' or the 'threat', rather than as bona fide members of the community. This, in practice and at an ideological level, constitutes a denial of basic citizenship rights to these young people. It transforms them from being citizens to class subjects whose only 'legitimacy' lies in their identification as 'victims'.

Whether it be punitive law and order policies, or more liberal efforts to resocialise young people through 'shame and reintegration' young offender programs (Braithwaite 1989; Cunneen & White 1995), it is the effects, rather than the causes, of youth marginalisation which are at the centre of contemporary state interventions in the area of criminal justice. Where issues such as racism, sexism or class inequality do rate a mention, they do so as a kind of backdrop to the real issue of how best to control young people. The overall emphasis therefore is on concepts such as 'social protection' (as justification for repressive measures), stigmatisation or shaming (in creating and identifying the 'other' against whom we are to be protected), and the entrenchment of social segregation (as a means to separate the 'rough' from the 'respectable').

The general tendency is for the state to use repression in the first instance, rather than as a last line of intervention. The coercive apparatus of the state is immediately and directly implicated in a project of overt class control, its targets largely confined to those who have suffered the most at the hands of an economic and political order which ostensibly says the market will provide for all.

VICTIMISATION AND YOUTH AGENCY

It is reasonable to ask at this stage how young people themselves are responding to the marginalisation process, and associated processes of rights stripping and criminalisation. After all, it is their lives, their experiences and their specific rights which have been so radically altered at a group level in recent years. The issue of youth 'agency' (that is, the conscious actions of young people in relation to the world around them) is intertwined with questions of analytical method and focus.

Certainly much of contemporary youth studies can be criticised for continuing to engage in a misplaced form of 'victimology', a sort of analysis which tends to separate out 'problem youth' from the rest of the population and from the wider structural determinants of their social positioning. Too often this type of analysis posits young people as simply passive recipients of whatever happens *to* them.

In a related vein, we can refer to the work of Palmer and Collard (1993, p. 119) who argue that the portrayal of indigenous people, and indigenous young people in particular, has tended to be based upon the acceptance of a number of popular misconceptions, and to be Anglocentric and victim-centred. They comment that a good deal of social research, 'often implicitly constructs Nyungar (Western Australian indigenous people) young people and their families as totally powerless victims who have had little or no agency, been unable to enhance their social position or had no capacity to determine their own futures'. They further talk about how the status of 'always victim' has had and continues to have major implications with regard to the exclusion of indigenous people in social research, including research about themselves.

The overriding impression of this kind of youth studies research in general is that young people can, and should only be, seen as 'victims'. Arguably, this type of approach was at one stage important politically, insofar as the stress on 'victim status' relating to homelessness, unemployment and poverty did for a time, at least in Australia, open the door to greater public resources being put into dealing with these types of issues. But the final outcome was less than advantageous for marginalised youth. For instance, where government action has been taken, it has tended to be extremely paltry and at the lowest levels of physical support for young people, rather than being more broadly developmental or structural in nature. While important and appropriate at specific historical moments, the rhetoric of youth as victim inevitably led to a 'welfarist' response on the part of the state, and accompanying this, ever more selective allocations of resources as definitions of 'need' and 'deserving' are used to establish that the money is indeed being 'well spent'.

It has also been argued that young women have been constructed as 'victims' of patriarchal practices. Recent analysis, however, has emphasised the agency of young women in interpreting and contesting social relations. The seemingly slow progress of equal opportunity strategies in having effects on the schooling outcomes of young women, for example, has been attributed to the fact that these strategies in practice operated within a discourse of young women as victims (Kenway et al. 1994). Unsurprisingly, young women do not appreciate being cast as victims of social relations of which, at the ages of 13 or 14, they are only dimly aware.

Alternatively, much of the recent work in 'cultural studies' has focused on young people as active creators of their social reality. The emphasis here has been on cultural dynamics and processes, which exist in a virtual free-floating state, and where young people actively pick and choose what kind of post-modern subject they are to be for the moment. Notions of class, gender and ethnicity fade away, insofar as the mode of communication—especially the mass media— becomes the central definer and template upon which identity is forged. Thus, self-image and self-identity are seen as reflections of process—a process in which young people attempt to manage the problem of 'how to invent and reinvent an identity out of a chaotic mix of consumer goods, advertising appeals and media cliches' (Hopkins 1995, p. 18).

In some cases, the analyst, as outsider to the youth identity process, is accused of constructing artificial and unauthentic identities *for* the young (for example, the 'homeless') and thereby seeking to impose their own form of 'governance' upon the young (Tait 1993). All knowledge is thus positioned within the same power dynamic, all labelling suspect because of its potential to exert influence and control. The problem with such abstract discussions of youth identity and sociological categorisation, however, is that it implies that process is everything, and that there are not real substantive differences between people. However, we do need some kind of structural explanation if we are to make sense of the concrete differences which have a habit of intruding upon our cultural creations. Furthermore, such studies move too easily from making universalising (and relatively uncontentious) statements, such as 'we all make our world through the conceptual categories we employ', to ones which imply that there is not therefore an objective 'truth' or 'reality' to which any of us can then refer.

Discussions of power, governmentality and identity which do not distinguish between different forms of power, but which rather concentrate on the diffuse sites of power, also make the mistake of overestimating the power which young people may actually exercise, and underestimating the importance of alliances between 'adults' and 'youth'. As Sercombe (1993, p. 10) puts it: 'Asking young people to fight their own battles is perhaps a bit hopeful or naive. This is especially so because they aren't young for long—just when they get good at it, it becomes someone else's battle'. It is important to acknowledge the liberating aspects of 'outside' intervention in young people's lives (for example, not all youth and community workers are engaged in negative or governance types of interventions). Likewise, it needs to be reiterated that in many cases the issue at hand is in fact not age-specific in any case (for example, unemployment or poverty).

Between the victim-centred approach, which sees young people as too passive, and the culture-centred approach, which sees young people as more constitutive of their reality than they really are, we would like to posit a view which says that young people do exercise agency, to varying degrees and under diverse circumstances, but this agency is subject to the pressures on, and limits of, activity arising from their material position and relations in society. The condition of marginalisation bears a number of collectively shared elements, such as lack of money, greater chance of coming under state surveillance, ambiguities in terms of how to forge a personal identity and social status, and psychological pressures relating to personal connection to institutions and feelings of powerlessness. How each individual responds to these elements depends upon the immediate situational factors affecting their time, space, activity, resources and identity (see table 7.1), and upon their own biography and psychological make-up. It is the latter which makes lived experience *contingent*, rather than simply a question of straightforward positive and negative experiences.

We can say that, of course, marginalised young people will be greatly affected by their circumstances. We can say that most experience life as a series of material, emotional and physical hardships, yet not without moments of joy, love, laughter and meaning. Crucially, however, while general threads of experience can be woven into a rather bleak and depressing picture, the overall detail is one which contains an enormously wide variety of activities and behaviour exhibited by marginalised youth. These include various forms of group and individual retreatism (such as substance abuse, suicide); progressive political activism (such as engagement in leftist and environmentalist action groups); gang-related activity (such as colour gangs or criminal networks); reactionary formations and activities (as seen in neo-Nazi, racist and homophobic attacks); and migration (within the same country, as well as between countries).

One response to the construction of urban fortresses and security zones for the rich, for example, has been the exercise of territoriality over the districts of the poor. Thus, the no-go zones of rich and poor are mirrored in the processes of fortification and ghettoisation. On the street, the marginalised, the dispossessed and those deemed to be 'social junk' are making their mark. They are taking back their streets, their spaces. This is achieved through force of sheer numbers. It is done through dance, graffiti and skate boarding. The message is the same: 'I am here, and this street, shop, building, train or tram is, after all, mine too'.

In the context of increasing economic polarisation and geographical concentration of the low-income and unemployed populations, the lived experiences of young people are also those increasingly signalling the general collapse of 'community'. For example, McDonald (1995–6) describes the social experiences of young people in the depressed western suburbs of Melbourne. In talking with young people, he was struck by the high levels of social disorganisation, and the personal angst and disorientation felt by many of the young people. Violence in the community is unpredictable and unintelligible. Petty theft is rampant. Pride of place and respect for one's elders is dissolving.

> Relationships of authority grounded in age and generation are giving way. It is the young ones who both tell their elders to get fucked, and who sniff paint. The older ones no longer recognise themselves

in this world that seems increasingly unintelligible (McDonald 1995 p. 20).

McDonald argues persuasively that the experiences of exclusion in terms of place and work amplify each other. The processes of fortification and ghettoisation thus ultimately have a very personal human dimension, and have profoundly disturbing social consequences for young people and other members of their communities. As McDonald (1995, p. 23) views it:

> The young people involved in this research are at the centre of a disarticulated postmodern experience: where community is undermined by disorganisation, where participation is blocked by exclusion, where an absence of social expressions of creativity is lived as fear, anger and loss of meaning.

An ethnography of 'marginalisation' thus reveals the pain, hopes, aspirations and bewilderments of living in a social world bereft of security, warmth and vision.

In the face of social censure via the media and politicians, and stepped up state and private policing, and in the light of basic material inequalities, is it any wonder that young people sometimes react in volatile fashion to their life experiences? The phenomenon of 'riots' is but a concrete expression of the explosive mix of economic marginalisation (for example, poverty and lack of welfare provision) and social repression (for example, racism and heavy handed police intervention). It makes sense that riots and varying forms of brutalisation occur in the crucible of disconnection and disempowerment.

CONCLUSION

A central feature of this chapter has been the underlying argument that to understand marginalisation we have to go beyond 'youth studies' analysis per se. For example, very often when people write about youth issues they describe the experiences of individual young people both in terms of personal problems, and the frustrations associated with age-based discrimination of some kind. With respect to the 'transition to work', for example, the following type of quotation is seen to be both descriptive and explanatory in nature; it tells us about immediate experience, and it contains within it the apparent reasons for the failure to achieve the desired end:

> I'm sick of doing courses because every time I try and get a job they say I haven't got enough experience and I've done all these courses, I've got all this other experience and they say you haven't got

enough experience. How am I supposed to get experience when I can't get a job? (SA 112 in White 1995).

The difficulty with viewing this young person's perspective as definitive of the problem, and its sources, is that while it is informative, it fails to capture fully the basic insights gained from a 'sociological imagination'. It seems to us that much more work needs to take heed of Mills' (1959) distinction between 'the personal troubles of milieu' and the 'public issues of social structure', and the relationship between the two in the case of issues such as youth unemployment, homelessness and poverty. In a word, it is essential to view youth studies research and scholarship as part of a political process in its own right. If we are to comprehend the myriad factors which together constitute the form of youth marginalisation, then it is incumbent upon us to probe more deeply into the nature of the wider social structure which fosters the processes of marginalisation in the first place.

The challenge, therefore, is to not lose sight of the whole pattern of a society in our quest to explain the circumstances of youth. Marginalisation, for instance, is part and parcel of a social polarisation under capitalism which disadvantages some while at the same time privileging and advantaging others. As Mills (1959, pp. 6–7) reminds us, the key questions are: what is the structure of this particular society as a whole? Where does this society stand in human history? And what varieties of men and women now prevail in this society and in this period? From our perspective the answers to these questions can, in fact, be found through an investigation of the life worlds and social circumstances of the young in our society.

The meaning of 'youth' achieves its best analytical value when it is linked to wider sociological theories of society, the state and human nature. Most of us can agree on the broad descriptive features of youth livelihood and experiences—the empirical trends relating to unemployment, poverty, ill health or homelessness, while not entirely uncontentious, do allow scope for general agreement among youth studies researchers that something is happening to and in the lives of the majority of young people. Similarly, we may agree on those aspects of 'youth' which are steadily being transformed by changing institutional arrangements and life opportunities. Thus, enforced and longer term dependency on the state and the family is presently being fostered by the extension of schooling, credentialism and an ethos which demands that we undergo permanent 'training'. It is being reinforced, as well, by low wages and social security payments.

In practical terms, however, we need to know what this actually means. How are we to interpret the marginalisation of vast sections of the youth population? What does the changing social content of 'youth' tell us about the nature of society generally? These are the essential questions of the present era.

By extrapolation, the search for answers to these questions can also make us rethink previous perceptions of youth. For example, the traditional notion of 'youth' was wrapped up in the socially constructed notions of less responsibility, less autonomy and greater dependency exhibited by young people from the turn of the century onwards. Yet, how meaningful are these categories when, in the end, they beg the issue of specific youth experiences, and the circumstances and lives of whole classes? Thus, what is the actual social position of young working class women when it comes to the dimension of 'independence' in relation to their typical future life prospects and communal relationships? Or, how does gaining 'autonomy' by engaging in paid work fit in with the concrete realities and relations of subordination, authority, exploitation and alienation associated with capitalist production methods?

The crux of this chapter is that before young people can truly be considered 'responsible' in and for their own actions, we must seriously tackle the question of the *responsibilities of society* and the state to the wellbeing of youth and in fostering the incorporation of young people into the mainstream of social life. But the chapter has also raised big questions regarding the nature of the 'mainstream' itself. It is to these issues that we return in the concluding chapter.

7 Conclusion

'Rethinking youth' is an important concern. Throughout this book we have argued that the concept of youth is itself problematic when it is used to categorise people by age alone. We suggest that placing the emphasis instead on youth as a *social process* offers the opportunity to understand how different social groups of young people face the struggle to reconstruct and define their identities against the more powerful definitions and constructions of other groups, including journalists, politicians, teachers and youth workers. Young people in post-apartheid South Africa, for example, face the difficult task of reconstructing their identities in a non-racist discourse. Similarly, young people in Nyungar and Koori communities and other indigenous Australians are working to strengthen the definition of their identities from their own perspectives, against the negative constructions placed on them by non-Aboriginal 'experts'.

Exploring social processes places the emphasis on the *relationship* between specific groups of young people and institutions, rather than simply describing the *effects* of these processes such as crime, deviance, antisocial behaviour, homelessness and suicide. This type of perspective offers an understanding of the politics of youth, a dimension that is of crucial significance to policy-makers, activists and practitioners.

We would argue that the issues raised in this book are not just about young people's participation in society, but about the extent to which *all* people are able to participate. Youth is a *relational* concept; youth is constructed in relation to adulthood. Our discussion of the fragmentary, unstable and disjointed nature of the

147

transitions to adulthood in industrialised countries challenges the notion that adulthood is a point of arrival. The very processes that have added complexity to the experience of growing up, such as unemployment on a wide scale, have also undermined the taken-for-granted meaning of adulthood. To the extent that full citizenship in society depends on having a legitimate livelihood, many adults are also being rendered marginal.

In our view, class analysis has a central place in any rethinking of youth. It is the pressures of and limits set by social division which frame the contours of youth experience and the shape of institutional and cultural processes with which young people engage. Youth and education policies which deny the relevance of class, gender and ethnic relations as relations of power in effect risk contributing to the production of unequal relations. The ideas of diversity, equity and difference which have replaced the language of social justice fail to grasp the *relationships* between rich and poor, success and failure, mainstream and 'at risk'.

The denial of the relations of social divisions has been legitimated during the 1990s by the resurrection of various forms of a *youth development* approach to understanding young people. The perspective offered by developmental psychology on the stages of development all young people must pass through has been central to the idea that there is a mainstream of young people, and that becoming adult is basically an 'individual' process. It is central to the reintroduction of standardised testing in schools and to the targeting of ever reducing funds to the most 'at risk' or disadvantaged groups. We argue that this approach has offered a perspective on the 'problems' of youth which systematically ignores the larger patterns, and focuses only on the outcomes of the processes of marginalisation.

Furthermore, we argue that the youth development perspective has been central to institutional practices which deny young people basic human rights—such as participation in decision-making and in democratic processes, and across a range of cultural, economic and political concerns. Young people must have their perspectives taken seriously. Every young person is entitled to the respect of others and to the recognition of their inherent worth and dignity as human beings. This demands that there be systematic institutional support and material resources committed to this end.

Research on the perspectives of young people indicates that an overwhelming majority want to belong in society, but that a significant proportion feel alienated and disaffiliated as a result of their experiences with institutional processes. Cultural studies have contributed to our understanding of how young people construct their identifies in the context of family relations, institutional experiences and social and economic circumstances. Analysis of *youth subcultures* explores the ways in which young people attempt to resolve contradictions of their age and situation, often producing distinctive perspectives and behaviour. In the 1990s it is the most marginalised who have the difficult task of reconciling the contradiction between the reality of their specific circumstances and the 'promises' of material wealth and wellbeing offered by an increasingly global society. In this context, the construction of identity is not just a matter of individual identity—it is clearly and fundamentally cultural, collective and political.

Discussion of institutional processes of *transition* demonstrates the profound disjuncture between education and employment for increasing numbers of young people. Education is one of the most significant institutions with which young people must engage. Although education is potentially 'liberating', the evidence is clear that schooling plays a significant role in the systematic marginalisation of young people who are poor and some groups of young women. It also contributes to racism. Understanding the processes of transition, then, involves understanding the interplay between institutional processes and the construction of individual identities and of cultural practices by young people. We argue that the concept of transition offers a deceptively simple notion of a linear and uni-dimensional process of growing up, which is contradicted by the experiences of young people as they move between education and part-time employment, unemployment and employment and other options in an ever extended process of 'becoming' adult.

It is important, therefore, to focus on the causes, as well as effects, of social division—the exclusion, failure and devaluing of groups of young people through systematic institutional processes. There are two central points in our discussion of youth marginalisation. Firstly, it is imperative to 'rethink' the concept of youth, acknowledging the significant differences between different groups of young people, differences which involve more than inequalities—they involve and reflect relations of power. The changing economic and political circumstances in which young people are growing up mean that it is even more important to understand the political and social implications of processes such as the privatisation of education, and of the assumption that market forces alone will offer young people (or, indeed, adults) a livelihood. The effect of these processes will be revealed in the 'society of the future' as social divisions are entrenched. But they also have an impact on young people's lives *in the present*, as young people negotiate and engage with class relations, sexism and racism.

Secondly, we argue that growing up is a process of forging particular types of *interdependencies*—in relation to other people and in relation to institutions. Conventional youth studies all too often frames the process of growing up in terms of a movement from 'dependency' to 'independence'. This not only ignores the actual experience of major sections of the youth population (for example, young women in relation to young men), but also presents a vision of humanity which is singularly insular insofar as it denies the ways in which people actually interrelate and rely upon each other. Conceptual terms such as 'independence' embody particular moral and political values which in the context of youth studies, tend to reinforce individualism and self-interest. Part of the difficulty with this is that it thereby excludes from analysis the centrality and dynamic nature of *social* relationships in the lives of young people. However, by focusing on interdependence, the emphasis shifts to the responsibilities of society for ensuring the conditions of wellbeing of young people and their active inclusion in the mainstream of social, economic and political life.

In this book we have affirmed the importance of understanding young people's experiences in the context of wider social processes. Being a young person involves certain elements in common, associated with cultural and institutional processes, but these common aspects of age are fundamentally shaped by cultural, economic and social processes. Youth research and youth policy, if they are to have any relevance, must acknowledge the tensions and contradictions between universal processes and particular circumstances and actions. Youth research has a significant role to play in revealing the social and political issues of the future, and in understanding these issues. But more importantly, youth research offers an understanding of the experience, meaning and significance of youth in present society.

Although young people are now acknowledged to be a significant group, they tend to be seen as people who will 'in the future' have a role in society. It will become increasingly evident, however, that young people have rights and responsibilities to participate in many aspects of society. *Participation* is the fundamental issue. A central factor which will enable schools to meet the challenges posed by increased retention and by student re-entry, is more *democratic* processes which will enable *all* students to participate in decision-making. This is fundamental.

The alienation of young people from the processes of formal politics also reflects young people's sense of distance from political processes that seem increasingly irrelevant to the lives of ordinary people (and especially to young people), and which seem to be increasingly exclusive. A significant dimension of democratic processes is the acknowledgement of inequality, of power relations, and of the rights of all groups to contest, contribute and shape the future. And the process begins at home as well as in the school.

A second dimension of participation is simply *equality*. All young people have a right to establish a legitimate livelihood and to belong in society. Economic policies alone are not enough to ensure this. Equality does not mean that everyone is the 'same', or that all outcomes from education, for example, should be the same. Equality, on the contrary, means firstly, acknowledging that advanced industrial capitalist societies systematically create inequalities in complex ways on a number of dimensions, and secondly, the maximisation of opportunities for the majority, which demands a more equitable redistribution of societal resources.

A third dimension of participation in society is the existence of effective *public* life: facilities, education, health care and accommodation. These are not just a luxury—they are a necessity to ensure that young people are able to operate in and contribute to society. The provision of a strong public sector is not just for 'disadvantaged' groups, it provides a basis for the development of active public life, politics and ultimately, for a society in which all people are able to participate as full citizens. The imperatives of social need, rather than private accumulation of wealth, should underpin economic and social policy.

The experiences of youth are diverse and complex. Cutting across this variation, however, are significant social processes which are affecting more and more people, young and old alike. It is our hope that by understanding the dilemmas and opportunities, divisions and commonalities of youth we are better placed to interpret the wider social world around us. And to change it.

References

Aggleton, P. 1987, *Rebels Without a Cause. Middle Class Youth and the Transition from School to Work*, Falmer Press, Lewes.

Alder, C. 1994, 'The policing of young women', in *The Police and Young People in Australia*, eds R. White & C. Alder, Cambridge University Press, Melbourne.

Allen, S. 1968, 'Some theoretical problems in the study of youth', *The Sociological Review*, vol. 16, no. 3, pp. 319–31.

Anderson, D.S. 1983, 'Transition from school: a review of Australian research', in *Youth, Transition and Social Research*, eds D.S. Anderson & C. Blakers, Australian National University Press, Canberra.

Anisef, P. & Axelrod, P. (eds) 1993, *Transitions: Schooling and Employment in Canada*, Thompson Educational Publishing, Toronto.

Ashenden & Associates 1992, *Listening to Girls*, Australian Education Council, Canberra.

Ashton, D.N. & Sung, J. 1991, 'Labour markets and the life course patterns of young adults in Great Britain', in *The Life Course and Social Change: Comparative Perspectives*, ed. W.R. Heinz, Deutscher Studien Verlag, Weinheim.

Batten, M. 1989, *Year 12: Students' Expectations and Experiences*, Australian Council for Educational Research, Melbourne.

Batten, M. & Girling-Butcher, S. 1981, *Perceptions of the Quality of School Life: A Case Study of Schools and Students*, Research monograph no. 13, Australian Council for Educational Research, Melbourne.

Batten, M. & Russell, J. 1995, *Students at Risk, A Review of Australian Literature 1980–1994*, Australian Council for Educational Research, Melbourne.

Beasley, B. 1991, 'Transitions to nowhere: the effects of government policies on young working class people's access to employment/training', in *For Your Own Good, Young People and State Intervention in Australia*, eds R. White & B. Wilson, Latrobe University Press, Bundoora.

Beilharz, P. , Considine, M. & Watts, R. 1993, *Arguing About the Welfare State: The Australian Experience*, Allen & Unwin, Sydney.

Bessant, J. 1993, 'A patchwork: the life-worlds and "cultures" of young Australians: 1900–1950', in *Youth Subcultures: Theory, History and the Australian Experience*, ed. R. White, National Clearinghouse for Youth Studies, Hobart.

——1995, 'The Australian juvenile underclass', *Australia and New Zealand Journal of Sociology* vol. 31. no. 1. pp. 32–48.

Blackman, S. 1995, *Youth: Positions and oppositions*, Avebury, Hants.

Boyden, J. 1990, 'Childhood and the policy makers: A comparative perspective on the globalization of childhood', in *Constructing and Reconstructing Childhood: Contemporary Issues in the Sociological Study of Children*, eds A. James & A. Prout, Falmer, London.

Brady, M. 1992, *The Health of Young Aborigines*, National Youth Affairs Research Scheme, Hobart.

Braithwaite, J. 1989, *Crime, Shame and Reintegration*, Cambridge University Press, Cambridge.

Brake, M. 1985, *Comparative Youth Culture*, Routledge & Kegan Paul, London.

Buchanan, J. 1993, 'Young women's complex lives and the idea of youth transitions', in *Youth Subcultures, Theory, History and the Australian Experience*, ed. R. White, National Clearinghouse for Youth Studies, Hobart.

Burke, G. 1983, 'Facts and faith in the economic analysis of teenage employment', *Youth, Transition and Social Research,* eds D.S. Anderson & C. Blakers, Australian National University Press, Canberra.

Carmichael, L. (chair) 1992, *The Australian Vocational Certificate Training System* (Carmichael Report), Report of the Employment and Skills Formation Council, National Board of Employment, Education and Training, Canberra.

Carrington, K. 1993, *Offending Girls: Sex, Youth and Justice*, Allen & Unwin, Sydney.

Castles, S., Kalantzis, M., Cope, B. & Morrisey, M. 1988, *Mistaken Identity: Multiculturalism and the Demise of Nationalism in Australia*, Pluto Press, Sydney.

Catholic Bishops Conference 1992, *Common Wealth for the Common Good*, Collins Dove, Melbourne.

Chisholm, L. 1990 'A sharper lens or a new camera? Youth research, young people and social change in Britain', in *Childhood, Youth and Social Change. A Comparative Perspective*, eds L. Chisholm, P. Buchner, H. Kruger & H. Brown, Falmer, London.

——1993, 'Youth transitions in Britain on the threshold of a "New Europe"', *Journal of Education Policy*, vol. 8, no. 1, pp. 29–41.

——1994, 'Contribution des approches culturalistes de la transition vers l'age adulte', in *Les relations entre education et travail en France, Grande-Bretagne, Allemagne et Italie*, ed. L. Tanguy, Armand Colin, Paris.

——1995, 'Problems and challenges in developing European youth policies', in *Growing up in Europe. Contemporary Horizons in Childhood and Youth Studies*, eds L. Chisholm, P. Buchner, H. Kruger & M. du Bois-Reymond, Walter de Gruyter, Berlin.

Chisholm, L., Buchner, P., Kruger, H. & Brown, P. (eds) 1990, *Childhood, Youth and Social Change. A Comparative Perspective*, Falmer, London.

Cohen, S. 1972, *Folk Devils and Moral Panics: The Creation of the Mods and Rockers*, MacGibbon and Kee, London.

Collins, C. 1992, 'The changing nature of the academic curriculum', *A Curriculum for the Senior Secondary Years*, eds T. Seddon & C.E. Deer, Australian Council for Educational Research, Melbourne.

Collins, J. 1988, *Migrant Hands in a Distant Land*, Pluto Press, Sydney.

Connell, R.W. 1987, *Gender and Power*, Allen & Unwin, Sydney.

——1993, *Schools and Social Justice*, Pluto Press, Sydney.

——1994, 'Poverty and education', *Harvard Educational Review*, vol. 64, no. 2, pp. 125–49.

——1995, *Masculinities*, Allen & Unwin, Sydney.

Connell, R.W, Ashenden, D., Kessler, S. & Dowsett, G. 1982, *Making the Difference: Schools, Families and Social Division*, Allen & Unwin, Sydney.

Corrigan, P. 1979, *Schooling the Smash Street Kids*, Macmillan, London.

Cunneen, C. 1994, 'Enforcing genocide? Aboriginal young people and the police', in *The Police and Young People in Australia*, eds R. White & C. Alder, Cambridge University Press, Melbourne.

Cunneen, C. & White, R. 1995, *Juvenile Justice: An Australian Perspective*, Oxford University Press, Melbourne.

Daniel, A. & Cornwall, J. 1993, *A Lost Generation?*, The Australian Youth Foundation, Sydney.

Davies, B. 1989, *Frogs and Snails*, Allen & Unwin, Sydney.

Davies, B. 1993, *Shards of Glass*, Allen & Unwin, Sydney.

Demaine, J. 1989, 'Race, categorisation and educational achievement', *British Journal of Sociology of Education*, vol. 10, no. 2, pp. 195–214.

Denholm, C. 1993, 'In: Red Hot Chilli Peppers, out: Jason Donovan: the current ins and outs of Tasmanian adolescent peer groups', in *Youth Subcultures, Theory, History and the Australian Experience*, ed. R. White, National Clearinghouse for Youth Studies, Hobart.

Department of Employment, Education and Training (DEET) 1989, *The Challenge of Retention*, Curriculum Development Corporation, Canberra.

Department of School Education (Victoria), 1992, *1992 Victorian Schools Survey*, DSE, Melbourne.

De Vaus, D. 1995, 'Adult–parent relationships: do life-cycle transitions make a difference?', *Family Matters*, no. 41, pp. 22–9.

Diamond, A. 1991, 'Gender and education: public policy and pedagogic practice', *British Journal of Sociology of Education*, vol. 12, no. 2, pp. 141–61.

Donaldson, M. 1987, 'Labouring men: love, sex and strife', *Australian and New Zealand Journal of Sociology*, vol. 23, no. 2, pp. 165–84.

du Bois-Reymond, M., Guit, H., Peters, E., Ravesloot, J. & van Rooijen, E. 1994, 'Life-course transitions and future orientations of Dutch youth', *Young*, vol. 2, no. 1, pp. 3–15.

Durning, A. 1990, 'Ending poverty', in *State of the World*, ed. L. Brown, Allen & Unwin Sydney.

Dwyer, P. 1995, 'Postcompulsory education in Australia and the domination of truth', *Journal of Education Policy*, vol. 10, no. 1, pp. 95–105.

Dwyer, P, Wilson, B. & Woock, R. 1984, *Confronting School and Work*, Allen & Unwin, Sydney.

Edwards, A. 1983, 'Sex roles: a problem for sociology and for women', *Australian and New Zealand Journal of Sociology*, vol. 19, no. 3, pp. 385–412.

Erwin, L. & MacLennan, D. (eds) 1994, *Sociology of Education in Canada, Critical Perspectives on Theory, Research and Practice*, Copp Clark Longman, Toronto.

Evans, K. & Heinz, W. 1993, 'Studying forms of transition: methodological innovation in a cross-national study of youth transition and labour market entry in England and Germany', *Comparative Education*, vol. 29, no. 2. pp. 145–58.

Fauske, H. 1995, Changing youth, transition to adulthood—the case of Norway, Paper presented at Youth 2000 International Conference, University of Teeside.

Finch, L. 1993, 'On the streets: working class youth culture in the nineteenth century', in *Youth Subcultures, Theory, History and the Australian Experience*, ed. R. White, National Clearinghouse for Youth Studies, Hobart.

Finn, D. 1987, *Training Without Jobs: New Deals and Broken Promises*, Macmillan, London.

Finn, T. (chair) 1991, *Young People's Participation in Post-compulsory Education and Training*, Report of the Australian Education Council Review Committee, Australian Government Publishing Service, Canberra.

Forrester, L. 1993, 'Youth-generated cultures in western Sydney', in *Youth Subcultures, Theory, History and the Australian Experience*, ed. R. White, National Clearinghouse for Youth Studies, Hobart.

Franzway, S. & Lowe, J. 1978, 'Sex-role theory: political cul-de-sac?', *Refractory Girl*, vol. 16, pp. 14–16.

Frith, S. 1986, *The Sociology of Youth*, 2nd edn, Causeway, Ormskirk.

Freeland, J. 1992, 'Education and training for the school to work transition', *A Curriculum for the Senior Secondary Years*, eds T. Seddon & C.E. Deer, Australian Council for Educational Research, Melbourne.

George, S. & Sabelli, F. 1994, *Faith and Credit: The World Bank's Secular Empire*, Penguin, London.

Gilbert, P. & Taylor, S. 1991, *Fashioning the Feminine: Girls, Popular Culture and Schooling*, Allen & Unwin, Sydney.

Gilligan, C. 1982, *In a Different Voice, Psychological Theory and Women's Development*, Harvard University Press, Cambridge.

Giroux, H. 1994, 'Doing cultural studies: youth and the challenge of pedagogy', *Harvard Educational Review*, vol. 64, no. 3, pp. 278–308.

Gottfriedson, M. & Hirschi, T. 1990, *A General Theory of Crime*, Stanford University Press, Stanford.

Graetz, B. 1992, 'Health consequences of employment and unemployment' in *Youth in the Eighties: Papers from the Australian Longitudinal Survey Research Project*, eds R.G. Gregory & T. Karmel, Centre for Economic Policy Research, Australian National University, Canberra.

Gramsci, A. 1971, *Prison Notebooks*, International Publishers, New York.

Graycar, A. & Jamrozik, A. 1989, *How Australians Live: Social Policy in Theory and Practice*, Macmillan, Melbourne.

Green, A. 1991, 'The reform of post-16 education and training and the lessons from Europe', *Journal of Education Policy*, vol. 6, no. 3, pp. 327–39.

Greer, G. 1991, *The Change*, Penguin, London.

Griffin, C. 1985, *Typical Girls? Young Women from School to the Job Market*, Routledge & Kegan Paul, London.

——1993, *Representations of Youth*, Polity, Cambridge.

Guerra, C. & White, R. (eds) 1995, *Ethnic Minority Youth in Australia, Challenges and Myths*, National Clearinghouse for Youth Studies, Hobart.

Hall, S. & Jefferson, T. (eds) 1976, *Resistance Through Rituals: Youth Subcultures in Post-war Britain*, Hutchinson, London.

Hartley, R. 1989, *What Price Independence?*, Youth Affairs Council of Victoria, Melbourne.

Hartley, R. & Wolcott, I. 1994, *The Position of Young People in Relation to the Family*, National Clearinghouse for Youth Studies/National Youth Affairs Research Scheme, Hobart.

Heath, S. 1995, Young people's expectations and experiences of leaving home, Paper presented at Youth 2000 International Conference, University of Teeside.

Heaven, P. 1994, *Contemporary Adolescence, a Social Psychological Approach*, Macmillan, Melbourne.

Hebdige, D. 1979, *Subculture: the Meaning of Style*, Methuen, London.

Heinz, W.R. (ed.) 1991, *Theoretical Advances in Life Course Research*, Deutscher Studien Verlag, Weinheim.

Hicks, R. & Moh'd, A. 1995, 'Islam & education', in *Ethnic Minority Youth in Australia*, eds C. Guerra, & R. White, National Clearinghouse for Youth Studies, Hobart.

Holden, E. 1992, *Getting a Life: Pathways and Early School Leavers*, Working paper no. 9, Youth Research Centre, Melbourne.

Holden, E. & Dwyer, P. 1992, *Making the Break: Leaving School Early*, Working paper no. 8, Youth Research Centre, Melbourne.

Hollands, R.G. 1990, *The Long Transition: Class, Culture and Youth Training*, Macmillan, London.

Hopkins, S. 1995, 'Generation pulp: entertainment and the postmodern generation', *Youth Studies Australia*, vol. 14, no. 3, pp. 14–18.

Irving, T., Maunders, D. & Sherrington, G. 1995, *Youth in Australia, Policy, Administration and Politics*, Macmillan, Melbourne.

James, C.E. 1993, 'Getting there and staying there: Blacks' employment experience', in *Transitions: Schooling and Employment in Canada*, eds P. Anisef & P. Axelrod, Thompson Educational Publishing, Toronto.

Jamrozik, A. 1991, *Class, Inequality and the State*, Macmillan, Melbourne.

Jamrozik, A., Boland, C. & Urquhart, R. 1995, *Social Change and Cultural Transformation in Australia*, Cambridge University Press, Melbourne.

Johnson, L. 1984, 'The uses of the media: an interpretation of the significance of the mass media in the lives of young people', *Discourse: the Australian Journal of Educational Studies*, vol. 4, no. 2, pp. 18–31.

Johnson, L. 1993, *The Modern Girl: Girlhood and Growing Up*, Allen & Unwin, Sydney.

Johnston, E. 1991, *Report of the Royal Commission into Aboriginal Deaths in Custody*, vol. 2, Australian Government Printing Service, Canberra.

Jones, G. 1988, 'Integrating process and structure in the concept of youth: a case for secondary analysis', *Sociological Review*, vol. 36, no. 4, pp. 706–32.

Jones, G. & Wallace, C. 1992, *Youth, Family and Citizenship*, Open University Press, Buckingham.

Kelsey, J. 1995, *Economic Fundamentalism: the New Zealand Experiment— A Model for Structural Adjustment?*, Pluto Press, London.

Kenway, J. 1990, 'Privileged girls, private schools and the culture of "success"', in *Hearts and Minds. Self Esteem and the Schooling of Girls*, eds J. Kenway & S. Willis, Falmer Press, London.

Kenway, J., Willis, S., Blackmore, J., Rennie, L. 1994, 'Making "hope practical" rather than "despair convincing": feminist post-structuralism, gender reform and educational change', *British Journal of Sociology of Education*, vol. 15, no. 2, pp. 187–210.

Kippax, S., Crawford, J., Waldby, C., Benton, P. 1990, 'Women negotiating heterosex: implications for AIDS prevention', *Women's Studies International Forum*, vol. 13, pp. 533–54.

Klein, H. 1990, 'Adolescence, youth and young adulthood, rethinking current conceptualisations of the life stage', *Youth and Society*, vol. 21, no. 4, pp. 446–71.

Krahn, H. 1991, 'The school to work transition in Canada: new risks and uncertainties', in *The Life Course and Social Change: Comparative Perspectives*, ed. W. Heinz, Deutscher Studien Verlag, Weinheim.

Kruger, H. 1990, 'Caught between Homogenization and Disintegration: Changes in the Life-phase "Youth" in West Germany since 1945', *Childhood, Youth and Social Change: a Comparative Perspective*, eds L. Chisolm, P. Buchner, H. Kruger, & P. Brown, Falmer Press, London.

——1993, 'Lurking vocations: girls' labour market perspectives and women's life course agenda', *Comenius*, vol. 52, pp. 410–25.

Lamb, S. 1994, 'Dropping out of school in Australia: recent trends in participation and outcomes', *Youth and Society*, vol. 26, no. 2, pp. 194–222.

Liebau, E., & Chisholm, L. 1993, 'Youth, social change and education: issues and problems', *Journal of Education Policy*, vol. 8, no. 1, pp. 3–8.

Livingstone, D.W. 1993, 'Lifelong education and chronic underemployment: exploring the contradiction', in *Transitions: Schooling and Employment in Canada*, eds P. Anisef & P. Axelrod, Thompson Educational Publishing, Toronto.

——1994, 'Searching for missing links: neo-Marxist theories of education', in *Sociology of Education in Canada, Critical Perspectives on Theory, Research and Practice*, eds L. Erwin & D. MacLennan, Copp Clark Longman, Toronto.

Looker, D. 1993, 'Interconnected transitions and their costs; gender and urban/rural differences in the transitions to work', in *Transitions: Schooling and Employment in Canada*, eds, P. Anisef & P. Axelrod, Thompson Educational Publishing, Toronto.

Lubeck, S. & Garrett, P. 1990, 'The Social Construction of the "at-risk" Child', *British Journal of Sociology of Education*, vol. 11, no. 3, pp. 327–40.

McConnochie, K. 1982, 'The concept of adolescence and desert Aboriginal communities', *Wikaru*, vol. 11, pp. 42–52.

McDonald, K. 1995–6, 'Morals is all you've got', *Arena Magazine*, December–January, pp. 18–23.

McDonnell, L., Harris, A. & White, R. 1995, 'Multiple Economies and Youth Livelihood', Unpublished paper, Department of Criminology, University of Melbourne, Melbourne.

McRae, I. 1992, 'Part-time employment: where does it lead?' in *Youth in the Eighties: Papers from the Australian Longitudinal Survey Research*

Project, eds R.G. Gregory & T. Karmel, Centre for Economic Policy Research, Australian National University, Canberra.

McRobbie, A. 1991, *Feminism and Youth Culture. From Jackie to Just Seventeen,* Macmillan Youth Questions, London.

McRobbie, A. & Nava, M. (eds) 1984, *Gender and Generation,* Macmillan, London.

Mandell, N. & Crysdale, S. 1993, 'Gender tracks: male–female perceptions of home–school–work transitions', in *Transitions: Schooling and Employment in Canada,* eds P. Anisef & P. Axelrod, Thompson Educational Publishing, Toronto.

Marginson, S. 1993, *Education and Public Policy in Australia,* Cambridge University Press, Cambridge.

Miller, P., Kim K.S. & Johnson G.M. 1991, 'The disappearance of childhood and the concept of children at risk', *New Education,* vol. 13, no. 2, pp. 25–31.

Mills, C.W. 1959, *The Sociological Imagination,* Penguin, New York.

Mitterauer, M. 1993, *A History of Youth,* translated by Graeme Dunphy, Blackwell, Oxford.

Monnich, I. & Witzel, A. 1995, The impact of local labor markets on occupational paths of young adults, Paper presented at the Workshop on Longitudinal Research on the Transition from Adolescence to Adulthood, Special Research Centre 186, University of Bremen.

Moore, D. 1994, *The Lads in Action: Social Process in an Urban Youth Subculture,* Arena, Aldershot.

Moss, I. 1993, *State of the Nation: A Report on People of Non-English Speaking Backgrounds,* Human Rights and Equal Opportunity Commission, Australian Government Publishing Service, Canberra.

Moysey, S. 1993, 'Marxism and subculture', in *Youth Subcultures, Theory, History and the Australian Experience,* ed. R. White, National Clearinghouse for Youth Studies, Hobart.

Murdoch, G. & McCron, R. 1976, 'Consciousness of class and consciousness of generation', in *Resistance Through Rituals: Youth Subcultures in Post-war Britain,* eds S. Hall & T. Jefferson, Hutchinson, London.

National Youth Affairs Research Scheme/Australian Bureau of Statistics 1993, *Australia's Young People: A Statistical Profile,* National Clearinghouse for Youth Studies, Hobart.

Nava, M. 1984, 'Youth service provision, social order and the question of girls', in *Gender and Generation,* eds A. McRobbie & M. Nava, Macmillan, London.

NYARS/ABS. *See* National Youth Affairs Research Scheme/Australian Bureau of Statistics.

O'Donnell, C. 1984, *The Basis of the Bargain: Gender, Schooling and Jobs,* George, Allen & Unwin, Sydney.

OECD. *See* Organisation for Economic Development.

Office of Youth Affairs 1978, *The Move out of School for a Group of Early School Leavers in Australia: A Study by the Office of Youth Affairs*, Department of Environment, Housing and Community Development, Canberra.

Organisation for Economic Cooperation and Development 1993, *OECD Employment Outlook*, OECD, Paris.

Palmer, D. & Collard, L. 1993, 'Aboriginal young people and youth subcultures', in *Youth Subcultures, Theory, History and the Australian Experience*, ed. R. White, National Clearinghouse for Youth Studies, Hobart.

Perrone, S. 1995, 'Workplace fatalities and the adequacy of prosecution', *Law in Context*, vol. 13, no. 1, pp. 81–105.

Pettman, J. 1992, *Living in the Margins*, Allen & Unwin, Sydney.

Poik, K. 1993, 'Reflections on youth subcultures' in *Youth Subcultures, Theory, History and the Australian Experience*, ed. R. White, National Clearinghouse for Youth Studies, Hobart.

Poole, M. 1992, 'Summary and conclusion: issues in need of policy formation', in *Education and Work*, ed. M. Poole, Australian Council for Educational Research, Melbourne.

Probert, B. 1989, *Working Life*, McPhee Gribble, Melbourne.

Probert, B. & Wilson, B. 1993, 'Gendered work', in *Pink Collar Blues: Work, Gender and Technology*, eds B. Probert & B. Wilson, Melbourne University Press, Melbourne.

Pulcini, T. 1990, 'A lesson in values conflict: issues in the educational formations of American Muslim youth', *Journal Institute of Muslim Minority Affairs*, vol. 11, no. 1, pp. 127–52.

Pusey, M. 1992, *Economic Rationalism in Canberra: a Nation-building State Changes its Mind*, Cambridge University Press, Cambridge.

Ranald, P. 1995, 'National Competition Policy', *Journal of Australian Political Economy*, no. 36, pp. 1–26.

Robinson, S. & Gregson, N. 1992, 'The "underclass": a class apart?', *Critical Social Policy*, vol. 12, no. 1, pp. 38–51.

Rose, N. 1989, *Governing the Soul: The Shaping of the Private Self*, Routledge, London.

Rosenthal, D., Moore, S. & Buzwell, S. 1994, 'Homeless youths: sexual and drug-related behaviour, sexual beliefs and HIV/AIDS risk', *AIDS Care*, vol. 6, pp. 83–94.

Seddon, T. & Deer, C.E. (eds) 1992, *A Curriculum for the Senior Secondary Years*, Australian Council for Educational Research, Melbourne.

Segal, L. 1990, *Slow Motion: Changing Masculinities, Changing Men*, Virago London.

Sercombe H. 1993, 'Youth theory: Marx or Foucault?' in *Youth Subcultures, Theory, History and the Australian Experience*, ed. R. White, National Clearinghouse for Youth Studies, Hobart.

Stratton, J. 1992, *The Young Ones: Working-Class Culture, Consumption and the Category of Youth*, Black Swan Press, Perth.

Stratton, J. 1993, 'Bodgies and Widgies: Just working class kids doing working class things', in *Youth Subcultures, Theory, History and the Australian Experience*, ed. R. White, National Clearinghouse for Youth Studies, Hobart.

Sweet, R. 1983, 'Changing patterns of work and education', in *Youth, Transition and Social Research*, eds D.S. Anderson & C. Blakers, Australian National University Press, Canberra.

——1992, 'Can Finn deliver vocational competence?' *Unicorn*, vol. 18, no. 1, pp. 31–43.

Tait, G. 1993, 'Reassessing street kids: a critique of subculture theory', in *Youth Subcultures, Theory, History and the Australian Experience*, ed. R. White, National Clearinghouse for Youth Studies, Hobart.

Taylor, S. 1993, 'Sub-versions: feminist perspectives on youth subcultures', *Youth Subcultures, Theory, History and the Australian Experience*, ed. R. White, National Clearinghouse for Youth Studies, Hobart.

Taylor, S. & Henry, M. 1994, 'Equity and the new post-compulsory education and training policies in Australia: a progressive or regressive agenda?', *Journal of Education Policy*, vol. 9, no. 2, pp. 105–27.

Teese, R., Polesel, J. & McLean, G. 1993, *Locational Disadvantage in Educational Outcomes: A Geographical Analysis of Curriculum Access and School Success in Victoria*, Youth Research Centre, Melbourne.

United Nations 1986, *The Situation of Youth in the 1980s and Prospects and Challenges for the Year 2000*, Department of International Economic and Social Affairs, New York.

——1993, *The Global Situation of Youth in the 1990's: Trends and Prospects*, United Nations, New York.

Walker, J. 1987, *Louts and Legends: Male Youth Culture in an Inner City School*, Allen & Unwin, Sydney.

Walker, L. 1993, 'Girls, schooling and subcultures of resistance', in *Youth Subcultures, Theory, History and the Australian Experience*, ed. R. White, National Clearinghouse for Youth Studies, Hobart.

Wallace, C. & Cross, M. (eds) 1990, *Youth in Transition, the Sociology of Youth and Youth Policy*, Falmer Press, London.

Wallace, C. & Kovacheva, S. 1995, *Youth and Society*, London, Macmillan.

Warner, D. 1992, 'The operation of a post-compulsory college', in *A Curriculum for the Senior Secondary Years,* eds T. Seddon & C.E. Deer, Australian Council for Educational Research, Melbourne.

Waterhouse, R. 1994, 'Third of UK youth in poverty: Report', *The Age*, 16 July, p. 7

Watson, I. 1993, 'Education, class and culture: the Birmingham ethnographic tradition and the problem of the new middle class', *British Journal of Sociology of Education*, vol. 14, no. 2, pp. 179–97.

Webster, S. & Nabigon, H. 1993, 'First nations empowerment in community based research', in *Transitions: Schooling and Employment in Canada,* eds P. Anisef & P. Axelrod, Thompson Educational Publishing, Toronto.
Wexler, P. 1992, *Becoming Somebody, Toward a Social Psychology of School,* Falmer Press, London.
White, R. 1989, 'Making ends meet: young people, work and the criminal economy', *Australian and New Zealand Journal of Criminology,* vol. 22, no. 2, pp. 136–50.
——1990, *No Space of Their Own: Young People and Social Control in Australia,* Cambridge University Press, Melbourne.
——(ed.) 1993a, *Youth Subcultures: Theory, History and the Australian Experience,* National Clearinghouse for Youth Studies, Hobart.
——1993b, 'Young people and the policing of community space', *Australian and New Zealand Journal of Criminology,* vol. 26, no. 3, pp. 207–18.
——1994, 'The problem of theory in Australian youth studies', *Discourse: the Australian Journal of Educational Studies,* vol. 14, no. 2, pp. 79–91.
——1995, Young people and the underground economy, Research in progress, Department of Criminology, University of Melbourne.
——1996, 'The poverty of the welfare state: managing an underclass', in *The State in Question,* ed. P. James, Allen & Unwin, Sydney.
White, R. & Alder, C. (eds) 1994, *The Police and Young People in Australia,* Cambridge University Press, Melbourne.
White, R. & van der Velden, J. 1995, 'Class and criminality', *Social Justice,* vol. 22, no. 1, pp. 51–74.
Whyte S. & Probert, B. 1991, *Young Workers in Technologically Advanced Industries,* National Clearinghouse for Youth Studies, Hobart.
Williams, F. 1989, *Social Policy: a Critical Introduction,* Polity Press, Cambridge.
Williams, R. 1977, *Marxism and Literature,* Oxford University Press, London.
Williamson, H. 1995, Status Zer0 and the 'underclass': some considerations. Paper presented at Youth 2000 International Conference, University of Teeside.
Willis, P. 1977, *Learning to Labour,* Saxon House, Aldershot.
Wilson, B. 1992, 'Full-time shifts: the effect of industry restructuring on young workers in full-time employment', *Youth Studies Australia,* vol. 11, no. 3, pp. 34–9.
Wilson, B. & Wyn, J. 1987, *Shaping Futures, Youth Action for Livelihood,* Allen & Unwin, Sydney.
Withers, G. & Batten, M. 1995, *Programs for At-Risk Youth, A Review of American, Canadian and British Literature since 1984,* Australian Council for Educational Research, Melbourne.
Wright, E. O. et al. 1989, *The Debate on Classes,* Verso, London.
Wyn, J. 1993, *Young Women's Health: the Challenge of Sexually Transmitted Diseases,* Research report no. 8, Youth Research Centre, Melbourne.

——1994, 'Young women and sexually transmitted diseases: the issues for public health,' *Australian Journal of Public Health*, vol. 18, no. 1, pp. 32–9.

Wyn J. & Lamb, S. 1996, 'Early school leaving in Australia: issues for education and training policy', *Journal of Education Policy*, forthcoming.

Wyn, J. & Wilson, B. 1993, 'Improving girls' educational outcomes', in *Gender Matters in Educational Administration and Policy*, eds J. Blackmore & J. Kenway, Falmer Press, London.

Yates, L. 1993, *The Education of Girls: Policy, Research and the Question of Gender*, Australian Council for Educational Research, Melbourne.

Yeatman, A. 1993, 'Contemporary issues for feminism: the politics of the state', in *Gender Matters in Educational Administration and Policy*, eds J. Blackmore & J. Kenway, Falmer Press, London.

Index

Studies in Society

Titles include: